A Note on the Author

Paul Dodgson is a writer, musician, teacher and radio producer. He has written extensively for theatre, television and radio. *On The Road Not Taken* is his first book.

ON THE ROAD NOT TAKEN

PAUL DODGSON

unbound

First published in 2019

Unbound
6th Floor Mutual House, 70 Conduit Street, London W1S 2GF

www.unbound.com

© Paul Dodgson, 2019

The right of Paul Dodgson to be identified as the author of this work has been asserted in accordance with Section 77 of the Copyright, Designs and Patents Act 1988. No part of this publication may be copied, reproduced, stored in a retrieval system, or transmitted, in any form or by any means without the prior permission of the publisher, nor be otherwise circulated in any form of binding or cover other than that in which it is published and without a similar condition being imposed on the subsequent purchaser.

Text Design by PDQ

A CIP record for this book is available from the British Library

ISBN 978-1-78352-775-5 (trade pbk)
ISBN 978-1-78352-777-9 (ebook)
ISBN 978-1-78352-761-8 (limited edition)

Printed and bound in Great Britain by Clays Ltd, Elcograf S.p.A.

For Poppy and Fred

Introduction

In the year 2000 my father contracted lung cancer. One day I visited him at Guy's Hospital in London after he had undergone a major operation. As we sat together by a window and looked out across the city, he began to tell me about an episode of his life I knew nothing about. It was the late 1940s, and he had recently qualified as an engineer with a love of mechanics and a passion for inventing new machines. He spent eighteen months in the city, employed by a Norwegian entrepreneur, designing a fabric printing press they hoped would revolutionise the clothing industry. As he spoke, it was as if his city came to life. I could see the bomb sites, feel the thick London smog, and I sensed his frustration at the machine that never quite worked. And that is when I realised how little I really knew about his life. Dad died soon afterwards and his stories died with him. He had never written them down. That is when I began to write stories from my own life and became interested in learning how other people had written theirs. One thing is certain: this is my story, told from my point of view, so to anyone else involved who sees it differently, I apologise. Most of all I realise this is a *story*, not a dry record of the facts. This means the past has been edited, significant events left out and others illuminated by research. Real life is often a messy thing that we might wish to be more like a story that adheres to a structure and resolves at the end. One criticism of stories I often hear when writing for radio or television is they should be more real. I suppose, ultimately, a memoir is an amalgamation of the two, creating a coherent story out of the messiness of life.

Writing this book has taught me so much about stories and the power of music. I am not only left with a renewed sense of awe and respect for the musicians who have walked me through the years, but also of how wonderful it is to make music too.

Islands in the Stream, 2013

On a luminous evening in May I take to the road, heading upcountry from Hugh Town to Carnwethers, stopping to watch swallows cut through the air over an abandoned flower field, the birds swooping low over untidy rows of daffodil stalks. The roadside verges are teeming with wildflowers and now the airport has closed for the night there is delicious music in the air, made of soft wind and birdsong. From high on the hill, I look across the ocean toward the silhouette of Bishop Rock Lighthouse, where the sea is sparkling and low sun ignites the clouds. For the last few years I've been coming to the Isles of Scilly on short teaching assignments and I love this place, twenty-eight miles into the Atlantic and seeming like a world apart. There are friends here, and tonight I'm headed for a party to mark two of them going away. Patrick and Lisa have painstakingly restored an old wooden boat and are about to sail off to another life on the mainland.

When I arrive, everyone is in the conservatory on the side of the house, so I let myself in, locate the booze table and open a beer. I am busy catching up when Lisa calls us to order. 'In Ireland, when we have a party, everyone sings a song. So I'll begin.' And she does with an Irish folk song that's unaccompanied, fragile and beautiful; no ornamentation in her voice, just a tune that carries the words, and the words tell a story. Others follow her lead. The owner of a guest house in town picks up a guitar and sings a few songs. They are simple and lovely, each new song a celebration. The music binds us together, turning the partygoers into a little community. It seems the most natural thing in the world until it comes to my turn.

'What'll you sing for us, Paul?' says Lisa. There is silence as everyone looks in my direction.

'I'll have to let this one pass,' I reply. 'I'm sorry but I don't have a song.'

It haunts me not to have a song. It haunts me late that night when I walk through the pitch-black lanes to Hugh Town. I think of all the chances to sing and never having done so. I remember, twenty years ago, staying at a hostel in Byron Bay on the east coast of Australia, and walking into a lush, subtropical garden full of backpackers talking, laughing and drinking. In the middle of the garden was a small stage with a PA where travellers could do a turn. I looked on as a young guy wandered on stage, bottle of beer in hand, looking as if he had spent the day surfing and had come straight off the beach. He was slender and unshaven with straggly blond hair and a faded T-shirt. Plugging in a guitar, he sang softly, close up to the microphone and, gradually, everyone in the garden quietened to listen. The sun was setting into dark clouds; there was a hint of sea on the breeze; there were lightning flashes from a distant storm above the hills; his fingers picked the strings; his soft voice carried through warm air. The young singer bound the moment together with his quiet song, so the sunset, the distant storm and all of us in the garden fused into a fragment of time that stands out from all the others.

As I think of it again, walking through the chill night air on Scilly, I remember how I wished, I really wished, I could walk on stage too. Not being able to do so haunted me then like it haunts me tonight. Why can't I? For the last thirteen years I have made part of my living writing music for theatre shows. I have written songs for other people to sing and yet I don't know any – mine or anyone else's – all the way through. I am fifty-one years old and in the far-distant back of my mind carry the dream of a troubadour life as I have done for the last three decades. And yet I can't even sing at a party. The truth is, and I can barely admit this to myself, I am terrified of singing in public, suffer from stage fright and, worst of all, don't really think I can sing at all.

Next morning when I pull back the curtains and look across the harbour, the haunted feeling is still there, and it stays with me when I take the little plane over the wild Atlantic to Land's End, and on the train all the way up the line to my home in Bristol.

Something has to change.

Puff, the Magic Dragon, 1967

This story really begins long, long ago in the south of England, in a town on the coast of the county of Kent. Today is a bitterly cold Saturday morning in the middle of winter. A lone dog-walker strides along the seafront with a woolly hat on his head, hands in mittens and a shivering dog on a quivering lead; in the High Street an old man pops into the corner shop for his morning paper and tobacco; in the church on the hill the ladies have arrived for the cleaning rota. Up the hill and back a bit is where we live in an avenue of modern houses. We came here when I was a baby and it is the only home I have ever known. On hot summer days we sit in our back garden and breathe the smell drifting over the town from the Mackeson brewery, or a salt sea wind from the coast, and we listen to seagulls shrieking, and steam whistles from the Romney, Hythe & Dymchurch Railway. But today is the middle of winter and my world is about to change.

Come into our kitchen where I am sitting at our yellow Formica-topped table, dipping a spoon into a milky bowl of cornflakes topped with white sugar. Mum is standing at the cooker over a pan of sizzling bacon, when Dad comes in with a scuttle of coke for the boiler. He stamps his feet on the doormat. I am happy and secure here, at the very heart of everything. The radio is on in the background. A song begins to play. I tune out of the kitchen sounds and listen only to the radio. It is as though I am drawn into a parallel world, the world of the song. It is that powerful. The song tells the story of a dragon called Puff and his friend who is a little boy. Soon 'Puff, the Magic Dragon' is the only thing I can hear. The words are carried by a melody that seems sad even before the story takes a sad turn. When the boy in the song grows up and forgets about the dragon, the happiness of the morning ebbs away like the tide going out on the shingle beach at the seafront. I don't know what has happened. How could a morning be turned on its head by a song on the radio? How can a song change the shape of a day?

This, this is what a song can do.

Alone Again (Naturally), 2013

The change, when it comes, is as sudden and unexpected as a punch in the gut. On a drab September morning I travel to London for a meeting. Afterwards, some of us go for lunch at a restaurant off Leicester Square, where the talk is of exciting new projects. The enthusiasm is so infectious, I end up leaving late, with just enough time get across London to catch my train to Bristol. Before I disappear into the Tube I check my email. There is a message from my partner, who is working abroad, confirming the end of our twelve-year relationship.

I am still staring at the email when we stop at Paddington. The doors open and shut and the train moves on. By the time I realise my mistake I am far up the Bakerloo Line and have missed the train home.

It is late evening when I step onto the platform of my station on the branch line out of Bristol. To avoid going straight home I walk over the level crossing and stand on the banks of the River Avon. The tide is out and the water trickles between mud banks as grey as slag heaps. In my mind low, ominous, synthesised drones are playing; dissonant and never ending.

When I can put it off no longer I go home. I unlock my front door and stand in the hall. The house seems different – somehow more empty – and I am aware of a soundscape barely noticed before, made from the footfalls of our cats on the wooden floors, the muted voices of children next door and tiny scampering of birds on the porch roof. I do what I have always done in moments of crisis and fill the silence by reaching for my guitar. The strings are old and lifeless, and because I haven't played as much as I should, my chord changes are slow and my fingerpicking clumsy. I run through a repertoire of songs half learned, songs half written: fragments of music, nothing complete. Everything has changed and yet everything is just the same. I want to find a way to turn these feelings into a song and come up with a phrase or two, but nothing sticks. It seems as though the soundtrack of my life is half written and half learned. My voice is an ugly rasp, but because the kitchen extends into the garden with no adjoining wall, the neighbours can't hear the racket.

In my kitchen no one can hear me sing.

Boogie Woogie Bugle Boy, 1967

After the breakfast things have been washed up, we put on our coats and get into our blue Morris Minor, which Dad carefully backs out of the driveway. We head along the seafront towards Folkestone, where there are big shops, and go for coffee at Bobby's department store in the centre of town. There is a big curved staircase leading up to the restaurant and Mum says this is very posh, as though we should be going to a ballroom on a cruise ship rather than a café in Folkestone. The restaurant is full of tables where people sit, talking quietly, with cups of coffee and wedges of cake. Also, there is a pianist sitting at a grand piano dressed in a smart jacket and bow tie. He seems to be playing songs, but they are more like a cascade of notes than a definite tune. I think it very rude that no one is listening, but Mum explains the music is for the background and not for people to actually hear. Despite this, I notice Mum and Dad speak in hushed voices just above a whisper. I can't imagine how music could ever be in the background, particularly when there is somebody playing it in front of you, so I sit and listen carefully. As the waitress arrives with the coffee, I am staring at the pianist, wondering how he can make his fingers dance at such speed, when he catches my eye and winks, then stops the cascade of notes and changes to a much faster tune. 'Boogie Woogie Bugle Boy,' says Dad. All around the restaurant heads start to bob from side to side and fingers drum the table. Dad's head starts bobbing too and he looks at me and exaggerates the movement, encouraging me to join in. Although I feel as though I am bobbing about inside, I am suddenly shy and sit frozen in my seat, unable to show how the music makes me feel, so it is a relief when the fast tune ends and the cascading notes return. I want to know if it is hard to play the piano and Mum tells me that it is and it takes many years of practice to be really good, but that will only happen if you have a musical ear. Mum says that Grandad had a musical ear and could play the piano well, although he never had a lesson in his life and couldn't read music. He even had a band with drums, banjo and a violin that used to play in their back room on a Friday night. Then Mum tells me something really surprising. She can play the piano too. I can't believe I didn't know this before. 'We need to get one then,' I say. Mum and Dad laugh. 'I stopped playing ages ago,' she says. 'Hardly anyone has a piano any more.'

Only the Lonely, 2013

For the first time in my life I am living alone. The washing-up starts to pile by the sink and I only pick up a dishcloth when there are no more clean plates. I empty my bags on kitchen surfaces and sweep aside piles of receipts, pencils and leaflets before making something to eat. There is a Co-op around the corner and I work my way through ready meals: lasagnes, pizzas and fish pies. I become a friend of the local fish and chip shop. But amid the gathering squalor I discover one real advantage of living alone: I can play and sing whenever I want and no one is listening. Late at night I sit in the kitchen and sing, filling the room with noise, and it doesn't matter how tuneless I am because no one can hear. All my life I've been conscious of someone listening and finding fault and now I can just sing. The writer, Lavinia Greenlaw, in her memoir *The Importance of Music to Girls*, says, 'We reveal something of our nature when we sing, something that can be disguised in our speaking voice.' Perhaps that is why I have kept my singing voice hidden for years and now in an empty house can let it all out. The kitchen is a good place to sing, because

12

the hard walls reflect the sound, supporting my voice, making it seem stronger than it really is. I run through the repertoire of fragments, recording them on my phone. When I listen back I am always disappointed, as though the voice I hear and what is recorded are different entities; as I sing I am Bruce Springsteen but when I play back I know I am not. Sometimes my voice sounds uncomfortable; sometimes the words land on the wrong beat of the bar; sometimes I am simply out of tune. But despite these faults there is pleasure in the act of singing: a joy in letting go, in making sound and music with my whole body. Very occasionally I think I'm getting better; a moment when the voice and guitar come together, when the rasping works with the fragment sung. Then I replay the sound file over and over again, trying to work out what I have done and if it can be repeated.

When I write music for theatre shows it is often my job to teach songs to the cast. I always begin by apologising for my voice. 'Sorry about this,' I say before singing the first line three or four times over. Very often an actor will squint while listening and tell me I have sung the line differently each time. Once, I recorded all the songs for a new musical the night before the first rehearsal. The next day I sat in a dusty hall with the cast, crew and theatre management for a read-through of the script. A great deal of money had been invested in the production so there was a lot at stake. When it came to a song I played the demos from my computer. As soon as I started the playback of the first number, I knew

13

I had made a terrible mistake, as what had sounded fine at home the night before sounded awful when amplified and played through big speakers in a rehearsal room. There were ten songs in total and time passed very slowly. We were sitting in a circle so there was no escape from watching everyone looking at their feet. There is nothing worse, I realised, than sitting among a group of musical people and subjecting them to out-of-tune singing ten times over.

Things improved once the cast learned the songs and the show picked up a good review in the *Guardian*. It was revived a couple of years later in the main house at the Theatre Royal, Bath. The first night was a near sell-out and when the final song ended I looked back at the stalls, circle, upper circle and the gods. Nine hundred people were applauding, and the sound of that was extraordinary, but then, one by one, the audience started standing up and cheering as well. And my songs were part of the reason this was happening. A friend told me she walked into a multi-storey car park on the way home where people were actually singing a song from the show. She said how lovely it was to hear such a happy sound echoing around the building. This was a glimpse of what things could be like. It was as though I had spent my whole life looking down a dark corridor towards a room full of light, then, just for a moment, I had been allowed in and could see what the room was really like and it was full of wonders.

My acoustic guitar sits on a stand in the kitchen, always close at hand, and I get in the habit of coming home, feeding the cats and singing a bit of a song. When cooking, I set a saucepan on the hob and play, looking down the garden and across to the wooded slopes of the Avon Gorge. I realise so much of my life takes place in the virtual world, where words are crafted on screen before they are shown. Guitar playing is something visceral that happens in real time; there are no edits or retakes, just the moment in which the music is made. As I strum, pick and sing, the colour of the trees turns from the dark green of late summer, to russet, magenta and gold. Through the steamed-up windows of midwinter I see the ghostly silhouettes of trees, until blue skies and fresh green herald the coming of spring. And when it does and I listen back to my recordings I realise I have improved. The progress is slight but it is definitely there. The singing sounds more tuneful and the playing more confident. It might only be a fragment at the moment, but a song has emerged from the silence.

American Patrol, 1968

I keep asking Mum and Dad about a piano but we never get one. Instead they save up for a radiogram from the electrical department of Bobby's. For over a year we look at different models on our Saturday trips to Folkestone, until one day I come home from school to find the furniture in the living room has been moved around. Now, in pride of place in the alcove is a large, rectangular wooden cabinet on legs. Mum allows me to explore as long as I am very careful, so I lift the heavy wooden lid to discover the secrets of the turntable inside. When Dad comes home from work, he brings out the one record we own. It was a Christmas present from Mum and it is called *This Is James Last*. 'It's jazz,' says Dad. On the front is a photograph of a man with a tweedy jacket, smart haircut and neat beard, who is leaning against his hand and staring at the camera. There is a look on his face somewhere between dead serious and a smile. Dad explains this is actually James Last and he is the leader of the band. When I ask what instrument he plays Dad says he is the conductor. Out of the sleeve comes a white paper cover to stop the record getting dusty, then out of that comes the record itself, made of black vinyl with a red label in the middle. Dad holds the record between his palms, only touching the very edge. He tells me the disc is full of little grooves and that is where the music is stored. 'You have to be careful not to touch them or they get scratched and that spoils the music.' There is a hole in the middle of the record and Dad puts this over a spindle on the turntable, before putting a plastic arm over the disc to hold it in place. 'It's automatic,' says Dad. 'Watch this.' He flicks a lever with his fingers and like magic, the record drops onto the spinning turntable, before a larger arm lifts and moves to the left, slowly dropping down onto the disc, where a needle follows the grooves. Dad, who is an engineer, thinks all this is brilliant. Out of the speakers in the front of the cabinet comes a crackling sound, then drums start playing and the whole band join in. I can hear trumpets, saxophones, trombones, a piano. The sound is bright and makes the living room seem different, as though it was dark and someone switched the lights on. For a few seconds Mum and Dad stand absolutely still, staring at the radiogram, shocked they have made this happen, right here in our house. 'This is called "American Patrol",' Mum tells me, her voice raised above the music. 'It used to be famous in the war.' Then Dad, who has started tapping his foot, takes hold of Mum's hand and they begin to dance, right in front of me. We listen to the record until it stops, then Dad turns it over and we do the same again. As each song starts to play they tell me what it is called –

'Greensleeves', 'Yesterday', 'I Got You Babe' – instrumental versions of pop songs we have heard on the radio. Also, there are bits of classical music that James Last has made jazzy: Bruch's Violin Concerto; the 'Toreador's March' from *Carmen*. Some are fast and some are slow but they all have the same bright sound. The music of James Last is definitely making Mum and Dad happy. At the very end is a song called 'La Bamba' with a very lively tune and I can't help having a dance with Mum and Dad, though not a real dance, more of a pretend version of someone dancing.

A few weeks later we are watching a variety show on our black-and-white television, when the announcer says the next act will be the James Last Band. We all lean forward in our seats. There are a lot of musicians on the screen and James Last stands on a little platform in front of them waving his arms. I want to know what the arm waving means and Dad says this is conducting, which is telling the musicians how to play. James Last has his back to the audience and every so often turns around so we can see his face, though he still waves his arms. Every time he does this he smiles in a way that doesn't seem real. I have noticed that whenever pop groups appear on the television, they always seem to be smiling and none of the smiles seem real. Mum tells me they probably have to smile to be on television and will stop once the cameras are turned off.

Lord Douglas, 2014

There are blue skies over Bristol as I walk down Park Street and into the garden of St George's, once a grand church and now a concert hall, and this weekend the venue of the Bristol Folk Festival. There is a bar in the garden selling real ale. Morris dancers sit on the grass in the sunshine with bells strapped to their legs that tinkle when they move. I buy a pint, go into the hall and find a seat near the front. First on stage is Jim Moray, who is only in his thirties and already a veteran songwriter, producer and interpreter of traditional song. I have been listening to him for years, partly because I like the way he is not bound by genre and has mixed folk music with electronica. One of his most popular songs is a folk – with brass, strings and massed voices – reworking of the XTC number 'All You Pretty Girls', a song so infectiously catchy it became a favourite of my children when they were young, requested as soon as they climbed into my car. With just an acoustic guitar around his neck, Jim starts to play an old ballad called 'Lord Douglas'. The song is a dark tale of forbidden love that ends with Lord Douglas dying of the wounds inflicted on him while fighting his lady's seven brothers and father, all of whom he kills. Lady Margaret dies of a broken heart, they are buried together and a briar and a rose grow out of their hearts. A virtuoso instrumentalist, he picks the tune with delicate flourishes and harmonies that make my head dance and send shivers down the back of my neck. It is so simple and yet the effect is so complex. I am moved and mesmerised by one man with an acoustic guitar singing an old tune in a new way and telling a story in a song. I had a moment of revelation like this in 1981 when I knew that singing songs with a guitar was what I wanted to do more than anything else. Now it is 2014 and I still have not done anything about it.

A month later I come home late one evening and open the doors to the garden. There is a rented house two doors up where a group of young Lithuanians are living. Whenever the weather is good they bring their speakers outside and turn up the volume on Europop – all bright preset synth sounds and autotuned vocals – so trying to sleep is like going to bed early at a festival. In fact, the only way to block out the sound is to stuff my ears with wax plugs, like I do at festivals. The housemates have not been speaking to me recently as they suspect I have complained to their landlord about the noise. They are out in their garden tonight, but the music is low and I hear laughter and the clink of bottles. It is one of those rare nights of early summer, when the sky is full of stars and the air warm and scented. The guitar has a couple of broken strings so I decide to replace them and go outside to play quietly in the dark.

I used to be wary of restringing and leave off doing it for as long as possible, but now I enjoy the process. It is a physical, almost sensual activity that requires a level of skill to make the new strings neatly wound and avoid getting fingers spiked by the string ends. There is a moment between the removal of the old strings and the winding of the new ones, when the guitar is like a wooden sculpture and you can see the fragility of the construction. I put my hands in places I can't touch when the strings are in place, like inside the body, to feel the texture of bare wood. Tonight, I wipe the fretboard clean as I have been playing so much that ridges of dead skin have built up behind the frets.

I sit on the step outside the kitchen door, pour myself a glass of wine and get ready. I have tuned the guitar to Open E, so when the strings are strummed, the chord of E rings out. In this tuning it is easy to sound like an impressive player, a trick I first pulled off when I was eighteen. I play a tune I wrote at school called 'Dalradian Moondance', the title of which is a long-forgotten joke involving geology and Van Morrison. With fresh strings, the guitar seems to come alive in my hands. I think no one is listening, but when I finish, there is a round of applause from two gardens away where their music has been turned off. 'Hey, you're good,' comes a voice from the darkness. 'Play some more.' I retune, then run through my fragments and improvise the blues. 'That is

21

great,' says the voice again when I stop. 'My dad plays the guitar too. You're reminding me of home.'

It is something to savour, sipping a glass of wine on a warm night and playing to appreciative strangers in a neighbouring garden. All I have to do now is be brave enough to sing.

Freedom Come, Freedom Go, 1971

We back out of the driveway. The air is thick with Elnett hairspray, the smoke of Player's No. 6 and *the tension*. Dad is in the driving seat, Mum is by his side and I am in the back of our new car: a green half-timbered Morris Traveller, which is like a mock Tudor house on wheels. Because of the cigarette smoke and hairspray I want to open the window. 'No, you can't open the window,' says Mum, 'I've just had my hair done.' If I was to open the window the rush of wind might spoil the hairdo. So the windows stay shut. Although we have no appointment to keep, Dad says we should have left fifteen minutes ago because of *the parking*, so now we are late and there is tautness in the air and a great puffing on the Player's No. 6. In a low gear we climb the hill by Sandling station. I look out to see the arc of Hythe Bay and the calm blue of the English Channel all the way round to the flat peninsula of Dungeness. They look too and the tension eases.

We have more records at home now and I have listened to Mozart, Beethoven, Bach and my current favourite, Handel. Apart from the songs on the James Last record, we don't have any pop music. Then, one day I am listening to the radio when I hear a song called 'Freedom Come, Freedom Go' by the Fortunes. Compared to Handel's Water Music, the tune is very simple, but it stays in my head and makes me want to hear it again. Next day I am in assembly at my primary school when the teacher says there's going to be a concert and she'd like volunteers to read something, play something or sing a song. I decide, there and then, I would like to form a pop group with my friends and sing 'Freedom Come, Freedom Go'. When I tell Mum, she suggests it might be easier if I read something from the Bible, because none of us actually play the instruments we need to be in a pop group. 'I don't think that'll be a problem,' I tell her. 'We'll learn.' Mum is doubtful, but says the first thing we need to do is buy the record, so that is where we are going now. This is the age before seat belts in the back, so I lie across the seat and look up to the blur of tree tunnels on Stone Street, the old Roman road that takes us to Canterbury.

The car park is half empty. We walk to Ricemans department store and pass through the perfumes and dresses to reach the record section. Mum and Dad have never bought a pop record before and don't know what to do next, so we hover by the record racks for a moment. The man serving has long hair. Dad would like me to go and ask, but I'm much too embarrassed, so we hover some more. Eventually, Mum plucks up the courage to go to the counter.

'Good morning,' she says in her poshest voice that sounds

like the Queen. 'Please may I have the record called…' She stops and sounds out the name of the song syllable by syllable. '"Free—dom Come, Free—dom Go", by a pop group called… the For—tunes. I believe it's top of the pops.'

Even at the age of nine I know how to be embarrassed.

Back at home, my two friends, Anthony and Ian, come for tea and a rehearsal. Anthony brings his recorder. We listen to the record and realise there are more members of the Fortunes than there are of us and a recorder doesn't appear on the single. 'Perhaps you could just sing it,' says Mum. We try but start on different notes and can't get beyond the first line without giggling. 'You could always mime,' she says. I have never heard of miming so Mum explains that sometimes the groups we see on television are only pretending to play and we could put on the record and do the same in the school concert. 'You could hold tennis rackets as pretend guitars,' says Mum. I think this is the most ridiculous idea I have ever heard. First of all the smiles are fake and now it turns out pop groups are only pretending to play, and as for us miming in the school show, I think it is a terrible plan. 'Everyone will know it isn't us singing,' I say. Mum says she knows they will, but it will be funny. 'I don't want to make people laugh,' I respond sharply. By the end of the rehearsal we have abandoned the plan to sing 'Freedom Come, Freedom Go'. Instead, Anthony plays a recorder solo, Ian watches and I read a passage from the New Testament.

A Rainy Night in Soho, 2014

The band come on as lager tickles the inside of my brain. Draining the plastic cup, I drop it and smile at Sarah, a new friend with me at the gig. Up on stage, close to the main microphone, is a pint of Guinness on a little shelf and we are close enough to see the colour of the creamy white foam on its head. Thousands of people are packed into this open-air amphitheatre, beyond which are the old steam cranes of Bristol Harbourside. A sailing ship is tied up to a nearby wharf, and in the distance are the flats where I lived when I moved to the city, twenty-five years ago. A curtain at the rear of the stage is pulled aside to roars of approval, and Shane MacGowan, in sunglasses, suit and dyed black hair, half stumbles toward the Guinness shelf, aided by a minder. After all the years of drunkenness and debauchery, it seems a miracle he is here at all. The band launch into the joyous opener, 'Streams of Whiskey', and all of us in the open air shake, jump and dance with abandon. The hot weather has broken, it is raining and I am sweating inside a cagoule, but the Pogues are in town and nothing can get in the way of songs that have been like friends for the last thirty years. It is dusk and before the audience disappear into the darkness I turn around to see the crowd behind me undulating like the surface of a sea; phones are held aloft, people are filming the stage and others are filming themselves smiling and singing along. So much time has been spent within a few miles of this place, carrying these songs inside me, and here are the band, a few feet away, bringing them to life. The songs of Shane MacGowan seem to evoke universal longings and desires. I love the characters who walk through his lyrics, the infectious Irish tunes and the rampant punk energy, still here after all these years. The first CD I gave my son was by the Pogues and they were the first songs he started to play on the guitar. I don't suppose my mum would think MacGowan has a *good voice*, but the beauty of him singing brings tears to my eyes, as it does during the encore, when the band play 'A Rainy Night in Soho', my favourite Pogues song.

It has been an exuberant evening, a celebration of being alive, but afterwards, walking into the centre of Bristol – now thronging with young clubbers whose nights are just beginning – I am aware that thirty years ago I would have drunk more, danced more, and felt more joy than I did tonight. Then, I would have abandoned myself completely to the music. Tonight there were moments of abandonment, but only moments, and even then they were guarded, as though I was watching myself in my cagoule watching the band. I am aware, too, that the stick-thin men who used to throw themselves about on stage are a memory. They are older and so am I. Time is passing.

Chopin Nocturne in E-flat major, Op. 9, No. 2, 1971

Soon after the 'Freedom Come, Freedom Go' incident, I decide something very important. I do not like pop music. When I think of everything I have heard on the radio or seen on television, I have never had another moment like hearing 'Puff, the Magic Dragon'. There was a man on the radio recently with a very deep, very posh voice who said pop music was, 'Bash, boom, crash,' performed by young men singing, 'Oh yeah, baby, oh yeah.' From what I have heard so far, I agree with him. Added to that, I don't like the long hair and the silly clothes. It all seems a bit *uncouth* and *common*, two words that are used a lot in our house to describe things Mum and Dad don't like.

When Dad is at work and Mum and I are alone in the house, Mum will often play a record of piano music by a composer called Chopin. When this is playing, I'll come into the living room and stop to listen. It sounds sad, but in a way that makes me enjoy feeling sad. Unlike a pop song, which seems to be the same tune all the way through, this music changes as it goes along, although you can always imagine the tune that began it all. The way this music makes me feel is the opposite of *uncouth* and *common*, so I decide to like classical music. Because this is something that goes down so well with grown-ups, I say I like classical music quite a lot.

Fairytale of New York, 2014

The song the Pogues do not play that night in Bristol is their biggest hit of all, 'Fairytale of New York', the duet between Shane MacGowan and the late Kirsty MacColl. It is a song born again every Christmas and marks the turning year. I used to think 'Fairytale of New York' could only be performed as a duet, until I went to a gig by the Irish folk singer Christy Moore and he sang a stripped-back acoustic version on his own. It was as if there was a song underneath the one I knew and I decided to learn it myself. For a long time, 'Fairytale' was the one song I knew all the way through. I used to play it to my children when they were little and they never told me to stop because it was full of funny words that made them laugh. When the children grew up and stopped asking for the song, I forgot the words. Now I have started to play 'Fairytale' again and once more it is the one song I know all the way through.

After the gig, Sarah comes to the house and we sit in the kitchen. My guitar is on a stand by the wall. 'I know "Fairytale of New York",' I say, and tell the story of how I only ever played it to my family, apart from on one occasion. 'When I say I've not played a song on stage for thirty years it's not strictly true,' I explain. 'It's just I was too drunk for it to count as a conscious choice.'

I used to produce the BBC Radio 4 request programme *Poetry Please*. The presenter – writer and broadcaster Frank Delaney – had just resigned because he was moving to the USA and I came up with the idea of recording the last three programmes in his new home country. I flew out to New York and on the last night, after the work was done, met a friend for dinner. After several gins and a bottle of wine we said goodbye and I took the subway back to my hotel. Walking through the lobby I stopped to look into the hotel bar: it was crowded with drinkers and full of laughter, and I thought it sad, on my last night in New York, to be heading for bed when there was so much life in the city. Then I noticed a guy in a suit, about my age, sitting alone at a table and looking back at me. In his hand he held a bottle of beer, which he raised, before taking a swig and beckoning me into the bar. I looked across the lobby to the lift that would carry me to bed and then back at the bar. I joined the guy. We started talking and I drank some more. After we had covered schools, jobs, families, music and the differences between America and England, he said, 'If you could do anything at all in New York, what would it be?' Without hesitation I replied, 'I'd sing a song in Greenwich Village.' In my troubadour fantasies, I had often imagined myself with a guitar in the

Village, the cradle of the Beats and Sixties counterculture. 'It shall be so,' said my new friend, and put on his jacket and led me to the door. I remember the swirl of lights as a yellow cab took us across town to a little bar with venetian blinds and a red neon light in the window. It was packed. A guitarist was on a stage in the corner, though he couldn't really be heard over the noise of people talking. In a gap between songs, my friend approached and whispered in his ear. The guitarist nodded and my friend turned around and gave me the thumbs-up. Everything seemed to be happening very quickly and I barely had time to notice how sweaty my palms had become, when the guy on stage held his guitar for me to take. I carefully put the strap over my neck, asked to borrow a plectrum and started to strum the opening chords of 'Fairytale of New York', hoping I could remember it from beginning to end. I was so drunk I felt I was watching a movie of myself. I stopped and started and juddered through the song. My voice and the guitar seemed to be extremely loud. When I came to the chorus – the bit about the NYPD choir – some people in the bar joined in and by the end loads were singing, although hardly anyone was actually looking at me. Then there was a cheer and someone thrust another beer in my hand as the guitar was taken away again. It turned out everybody in the bar was from one big Irish family who had come over for a wedding, and they were all very drunk too, so the poor quality of my performance had gone unnoticed; they were just happy to hear a song from home. My friend and I ended up in George Washington Park, looking at the arch that was the backdrop for the City of New York Police Pipe Band to perform in the video of 'Fairytale'. Looking through the arch I could see the lights of the Empire State Building winking in the distance, while Manhattan glittered like a starlit sky. Travelling to JFK on the bus the next day, hungover and weary, the whole thing seemed as weird and unlikely as a dream.

'Will you sing it for me?' says Sarah, after I finish the story. There is a threshold to cross and here it is, right in front of me. Unlike the New York incident, which just sort of happened, I can make a choice right now. Part of me wants to make the same old excuses: I don't know it any more; it's late; I'm tired. Instead, I pick up the guitar, put the strap around my neck and lean back against a kitchen cupboard. As I play the opening chords I look at the clutter on the table, my reflection in the window and Sarah, a couple of feet away, looking up at me. I feel exposed under the glare of the overhead light, so shut my eyes, take a deep breath, open my mouth and sing.

Twinkle, Twinkle, Little Star, 1972

I am standing in the corridor of my grandparents' bungalow in Broadstairs. Dad puts his finger up to his mouth telling me to be quiet as I lay the case on the floor, undo the clips, take the bow from the lid and go through the ritual of tightening and rubbing resin on the horsehair. 'Leave it for a minute and then begin,' whispers Dad before going into the living room where everyone is having tea. I count up to sixty, repeating the word elephant after each number to help me time the seconds accurately. While I do, I look at the picture on the wall in front of me, of a strange-looking ship sailing past jagged mountains. Grandma told me the boat is called a junk and the picture is made from cork, which comes from the bark of a tree. After sixty elephants I lift the violin from the green velvet lining and place it on my neck, bringing my head onto the chin rest. This is different from playing at home and different from playing in front of my violin teacher. This is a performance. My bowing arm hovers over the strings before I play 'Twinkle, Twinkle, Little Star'. The sound that comes from the violin only vaguely resembles the tune.

At home there had been talk of me learning to play a musical instrument for years. At one point our whole class started to have recorder lessons and Mum and Dad bought me one of my own, but I didn't like the sound and mucked about until I was told to sit still and be quiet. Then one day in assembly, we were told a violin teacher would be coming to school to give lessons. I wanted to learn the violin because my friends were and I didn't want to be left out. Mum and Dad were not so sure. Mum said the violin was very hard to play and would require a huge amount of practice, which she was not convinced I would actually do. Dad said I would need to be disciplined, really self-disciplined in order to progress, but that in itself was a good thing, for I would need to be self-disciplined to get on in life. Mum and Dad did not have money to waste, they told me, and violin lessons were expensive, so, if they agreed, then I must promise to work hard and practise every day. I promised I would, just like when I learned to tie my shoelaces. That was hard too, so Dad made a practice shoe out of cardboard and although it was difficult, really difficult, I got there in the end. Then there was learning to ride a bike. I remember the months with stabilisers and how frustrated I was when my friends had theirs removed and could freewheel, leaning and cornering, while I was slowed by the babyish wheels that left me lagging behind. Then, one winter afternoon, Dad asked if I wanted to practise in the garden. I put on my coat and gloves and went outside to see the stabilisers had been removed. 'I can easily put them back on,' said Dad, 'but I think you're ready.' I started to pedal in big, slow circles while Dad ran alongside holding me upright. Then he loosened his grip until he let go altogether and I was on my own, balancing, riding around the garden and feeling as though the world was opening up before me.

'Surely the violin can't be any harder than the things I've learned already?'

'It is,' said Mum.

The name of my teacher is Miss Curl, who has dark hair that actually curls on her shoulders, which I think is funny. She is young and can be very strict if I don't do as I'm told, so I pay attention to everything she says. We have rented a violin instead of buying one, so the money won't have been wasted if I give up. At my first lesson I explain I'm left-handed and expect to do everything the other way around. 'No,' says Miss Curl. 'You hold the violin the same as a right-handed person.' To begin with we practise standing in the correct position and balancing the bow. It feels awkward and unnatural. The hardest thing is controlling my right hand that never does what I want, no matter how hard I try. I practise every day after school, enjoying the ritual of preparation: getting out the violin; positioning music on the stand; understanding the symbols on manuscript paper in front of me. I struggle to learn the scale of G major but persist. My homework one week is to learn 'Twinkle, Twinkle, Little Star'. My dad, who has never played a musical instrument and has been listening to the scraping from my bedroom, is amazed that a tune has emerged, and suggests I should surprise my aunties, uncles and grandparents with a secret performance when we meet the following weekend.

Standing in the corridor I concentrate really hard, thinking of everything I should be doing: the position of my left hand; the position of my chin; the light touch needed to bow the strings. But it feels as though I am fighting my way through each of the notes of 'Twinkle, Twinkle, Little Star'. The talking in the living room stops and there is silence. Then I hear one of my aunties giggling, then an uncle laughing and turning the laugh into a cough. Dad opens the door so everyone inside can see me in the corridor. As I play I glance into the room and see tears in my auntie Winnie's eyes as she looks at me for a second, and straight away looks down at the carpet. My uncle Dave has a handkerchief over his face and my auntie Doris and uncle George are staring straight at me but look as if they are chewing the inside of their mouths. Only my grandma and grandad look normal, smiling at me encouragingly. When I get to the end, my dad, whose face and neck are very red – which only happens when he is cross – starts to clap a bit too loudly and everyone else joins in, though I hear my uncle Dave cough the words 'strangulated cat', which makes the aunties laugh out loud and pull handkerchiefs out of their handbags to dab their faces. No one mentions the violin for the rest of our visit and on the way home Dad tells me the aunties and uncles are rude and he is very angry.

Boulder to Birmingham, 2014

At the end of 'Fairytale of New York' I open my eyes and Sarah is still there. 'Fairytale' is not a hard song to play but is full of quick chord changes. I was confused partway through but found my way back again without stopping and making a big deal of the mistake. Sarah responds with a little clap and I take off the guitar quickly, explaining the extent of my repertoire is this one song, while secretly wishing I could keep going for hours. But when I wake up the next day something has shifted. I realise that one of the reasons I had not sung in front of anyone was my need to be perfect when I did. In her book *Playing Scared: My Journey Through Stage Fright*, the writer Sara Solovitch researches performance anxiety to understand why she has not fulfilled her potential as a pianist. Her investigation recognises the problem of perfection. 'No one can attain mastery in any discipline without a relentless drive for excellence. But the line between excellence and perfection is a thin one, and a body of research shows that it's the people most preoccupied with perfection that are the most vulnerable in performance.' Today perfection doesn't seem to matter so much, which comes as a relief. Also, I realise that a song only truly comes alive when sung in front of someone else, whether it goes well or badly.

If my singing ambition is to go any further, I am going to have to put in the work while facing the possibility of failure. All the time I sing to myself, I can continue the fantasy of being a mere step away from success. How many times have I been stopped in my tracks by a song and thought, 'I could do that too, if only I made a little effort?' Singing 'Fairytale' makes me realise how much I want to sing songs out loud in front of other people, but how much work there is before I am in a position to do so.

Alone again in my kitchen with the guitar, I make a start by learning songs all the way through. I print lyric sheets from the internet and carry them with me, learning a verse when I have a few minutes spare on a bus, train or in a café. I begin work on a new play for BBC Radio 4 and set a word count to reach, after which I allow fifteen minutes in the kitchen with the guitar. I sing whole songs and not fragments.

While away for a few days I learn the words of 'Our Town' by Iris Dement, a bittersweet country song about an adult leaving the place she grew up. When I come back and sing the song out loud, I realise it is in the wrong key for my voice. Then I make a startling discovery. Almost all songs, as they are recorded, seem to be in the wrong key for my voice, but if I put a capo on the neck of the guitar and play around with the chords, then I find a key that works. I really should have known this, but had been too busy believing I simply couldn't sing. The capo – a spring-loaded metal bar – opens up a new world of possibility.

'Boulder to Birmingham', by Emmylou Harris, is a song I have loved since hearing a version by the singer Christine Collister. I first saw Christine in the late Eighties when she sang in an acoustic duo with the prodigious guitarist and songwriter Clive Gregson. At the time I was living in a little room off Baker Street and walked through a blizzard in London to the Queen Elizabeth Hall where their record company were putting on a night of acts on the label. The snow had nearly shut down the city and the hall was only half full. Christine was tiny, but her voice sounded like it came from someone five times her size, and had that elusive quality best described as *soul*; a depth that would make it moving if she sang the menu of a fish and chip shop. Years later when I wrote a radio play that needed songs sung by an amazing singer, I tracked Christine down and asked her. The BBC hired St George's Hall for the day – the place that would later host the Bristol Folk Festival – and I persuaded Jason Rebello, jazz prodigy and member of Sting's touring band, to play the grand piano. I recorded the songs on cassette and sent them to Jason and Christine to learn. I was embarrassed by my singing and started the session with an apology, which was ignored as they got to work shifting keys and creating an arrangement. After the session we went for a cup of tea in a nearby café and when Christine tried to persuade Jason to collaborate on songs for her next album, I muscled in on the conversation and said I would like to do that myself. She couldn't really object. A month later, I sat down in Christine's flat in North London with a guitar and a few spare hours. A review in *The Times* once described her as having 'a voice personally delivered by God', so actually being in the same room as this voice made it impossible for me to sing out loud. I would suggest phrases and lines, but when I tried to sing them, nothing but a disfigured croak came out. Somehow we wrote a song that afternoon and when Christine's partner – a mover and shaker in the music business – arrived home, she sang it to him and he liked it. 'Ashlands' became the first track on the album *Into the Light* and I got to sign a publishing contract with Topic Records. Which was why, in 2002, I was at Cheltenham Town Hall to hear the song played live. It was a wonderful thing to hear 'Ashlands' introduced with me as co-writer, and then played to an audience. What had started as a phrase I had borrowed from a friend had become a living thing reaching out to the audience in the hall and travelling around the world on a CD. But it was the next song in the set that took my breath away. I didn't know exactly what Emmylou Harris meant by the lyrics of 'Boulder to Birmingham' and yet I understood it completely. It is a song of love, loss and longing, full of powerful images of canyons and prairies, evoking the bigness of the American continent. The lyrics are wrapped in a mix of major and minor chords that build to a chorus, allowing a singer to let rip and show

41

the power of their voice. When Christine sang the song that night it made me shiver in my seat. I never thought it was a song I could sing.

Then one afternoon I am cycling along home on the path by the river, looking at rock formations in the Avon Gorge and the sky above, when a line from 'Boulder to Birmingham' flashes through my mind and the song becomes the soundtrack to my ride. When I get home I need to listen to it properly. There is a particular chord change I can't identify and wonder what it is. These days such things are easy to find as so much music has been transcribed and put online. With the lyrics and the chords in front of me I decide to try singing the song. I move the capo up and down the neck of the guitar until I find a place where the opening line feels comfortable, and begin. To start with, all I can hear are the voices of Emmylou Harris and Christine Collister, but these fade away and my own voice takes over. I record the song on my phone and play it back the next day. For the first time in my life I can bear to hear me sing. I sound like me.

I'm on My Way to a Better Place, 1973

In the months that follow I try really hard, but of the group who started at the same time, I am the worst. The violin, I realise, is much harder to learn than tying shoelaces or riding a bike. In school assembly, children who are learning instruments are sometimes asked to play a tune to show their progress. I am never invited to perform. There is talk of the Grade One exam, but while others are put forward, it is decided I should carry on with the basics. When I eventually take my exam others are already on Grade Three. Practice has become a chore and I have to be told to do it. I do not like being the worst at the violin and because I feel so bad at it, begin to think that I'm not very good at music at all.

We are in the last days of primary school now and I am wondering what will happen next. Where we live, the clever boys go to the Harvey Grammar School and everyone else goes to Brockhill Secondary Modern. The girls are split up too and have their own grammar and secondary modern, plus one in the middle called a technical school. My friend Anthony is better at me than playing the violin but has already decided to give up. He can't see the point in it, but his mum and dad want him to carry on with lessons until he changes school. One afternoon, after Christmas, it snows and we look out of the window to watch a thick layer of powdery whiteness cover the playground, school buildings, trees and playing field. There is a slope between the playground and the playing field and after school Anthony wants to go sledging. 'Let's use our violin cases as sledges,' he says, sitting on his wooden case and launching himself down the slope. The violin case makes a terrible sledge, embedding itself in the fresh snow after a couple of feet, but it's so funny to watch we both roll around in the snow laughing, until we hear someone banging on a window in the new building. We look up to see Miss Curl, waving her arms and shouting. The windows are double glazed so we can't hear what she is saying, just mouthing words and pointing, which is even funnier. We grab our violin cases and run away across the snowy field like outlaws.

One morning next spring, Dad reads the letter that says I have not been selected for grammar school and must go to Brockhill Secondary Modern. I am holding a piece of toast in front of my mouth and it stays there as Dad reads the letter again. The word Brockhill always stirs up a feeling of dread, because of the tough-looking kids who tumble past me on their way home every day. Dad sets up a committee with other parents and appeals to the Council of Heads. We have laughed about this name, imagining a load of heads without bodies, but when a letter arrives from the appeal and I make the same joke again, Dad doesn't find it funny any more. 'This is nothing to laugh about,' says Dad. 'What this means…' And I see him trying to think of the right words. 'What this means is you might not have so many choices later on.'

Then it is the last day at Saltwood Primary School. I didn't think this would ever happen to me because time itself was so slow I would be at my little school for ever. After we put our chairs on our desks for the very last time, I go to the sweet shop next door with my friends Ian and Anthony. We have saved twenty new pence each and mark the occasion with a huge bag of liquorice, chews and sherbet fountains, which we eat on our favourite bench under the trees in Brockhill Road. I hand back the violin without any regret. Despite the sledging incident and my lack of progress, Miss Curl had tried to persuade me to carry on learning. I was almost convinced until she said the violin was not taught at Brockhill, as the headmaster preferred instruments that could be played in the army cadet band, like trumpets and snare drums. In order to carry on I would have to go to the girls' school for lessons. I am eleven years old and cannot imagine anything worse.

I Just Don't Know What to Do With Myself, 2015

I know I have drunk too much coffee as I pick up the guitar. I am twitchy and jumpy and don't stop to think. It is a Saturday afternoon in January and one of those days with loads to do and nothing achieved. In the past months I have worked hard learning songs all the way through and now have a small repertoire that includes 'A Rainy Night in Soho' and a brace of old folk songs, though nothing has travelled beyond the kitchen walls. In addition to the guitar, I have begun to experiment with a shruti box – an instrument from India that uses bellows to generate drones and single chords – to sing a song from Kent called 'Coal Not Dole', written during the miners' strike in the 1980s. To keep an eye on progress I have been propping up an iPad in the kitchen and filming myself. The recording happens at odd moments with a few minutes spare, so looking back I watch myself in a dressing gown, running gear and on one occasion a pair of pants, my unshaven face looming close as I start the recording, squinting at the screen to check it's working, then moving into position and adopting an awkward posture before launching into song. Although the sound of the singing is slowly improving, none of it looks very impressive. I see strange jerky movements and random head twitches. I think, 'Who would ever want to watch this?' I have also bought a set of harmonicas and a neck harness, wanting to be like every acoustic singer-songwriter back through the years to Bob Dylan and Woody Guthrie before him. On this dark January afternoon I come into the kitchen intending to wash up, am distracted by a pile of unopened post and then, seeking further distraction from an unpaid bill, switch on the kettle to top up the coffee pot. I plan to run through a song while waiting for it to boil. There is a simple order of events to putting on the guitar: lifting it from the stand with my left hand, putting the strap around my neck with my right, feeling the button at the end of the soundbox to make sure the strap is securely fastened and starting to play. With the addition of the harmonica, there is a new stage to the process: after checking the strap is securely fastened, I lift the harness around my neck. This afternoon, racing against the clock to play something before the kettle boils, I put the harness on first, lift the guitar over the top, and instead of checking the button, adjust the harmonica.

First there is a sense of weightlessness, then a moment of silence, then the sound of dissonance and splintering wood as the guitar hits the floor. I shut my eyes as the kettle reaches the boil and clicks off over the fading discord of detuned

47

strings. I turn over the guitar to see an ugly wound where the body is broken. The bracing and inner woodworking, normally hidden within the dark interior, are exposed to daylight and look like the shattered roots of an upturned tree.

I'm the Leader of the Gang (I Am), 1973

Ever since I was little, Mum and Dad have encouraged me to spend time with my cousin Nick who is a year older. This is because I do not have any brothers or sisters and am never allowed to forget it. They think if I share things with my cousin I won't become a spoiled child. I now think about Nick in the same way my friends think about their brothers, although we never argue or fight in the way my friends do with their siblings. It is now the middle of the long summer holiday and we are spending a week together at his house in Welwyn Garden City. One evening after tea, Nick and his younger brother Dave ask if the television can be switched on so they can watch *Top of the Pops*. This is a programme I have heard about but never seen. My auntie Shirley and uncle Dennis agree, and Nick and Dave settle themselves in front of the screen while I remain safely on the other side of the room. I watch with horror as a carnival of flared trousers, platform shoes and long hair appears in the room before me. Nick and Dave like some groups and not others. When someone they like comes on they get up and dance around the room. I cannot believe it. It is horrible. I say, 'None of these people can sing,' which is what Mum says when one of these groups comes on to the television at home. This makes everyone laugh, though Uncle Dennis, who knows about classical music, takes me seriously and asks what composer I like best. 'Beethoven,' I say. 'That's proper music.' And everyone laughs again. There is a big fuss made about what is number one in the charts and Nick and Dave seem really interested, though I could not care less, especially when the number one turns out to be a song called 'I'm the Leader of the Gang (I Am)' by Gary Glitter. Everyone seems to be enjoying themselves, so I do not say that I think Gary Glitter looks ridiculous in his high-heeled shoes, strutting and pouting to the camera and singing a stupid song about being in a gang. I do not like gangs, I do not like pop music and I do not like Gary Glitter.

Back at home the holidays are coming to an end. We drive into Folkestone because Mum and Dad want to buy a briefcase for all the books I will carry around at my new school. Inside a dark shop, stacked up to the ceiling with trunks, suitcases and bags, a fast-talking salesman persuades Mum and Dad to buy me a brown leather case that is much more expensive than they had planned. As I stand holding my new briefcase the salesman says, 'He'll still be carrying that when he starts at his office.' I am confused. Is this what will definitely happen, that I will go to work in an office? And how does he know?

Then it is the start of September and at half past eight in the morning, I say goodbye to Mum and walk down the avenue clutching my brand-new briefcase and wearing a smart blazer, new trousers and shiny shoes. I walk up the footpath between the houses, through Saltwood village and on to Sandling Road. The pavements are crowded with boys heading in the same direction all trying to cluster together on the same strip of path. Coaches drive past on their way to St Leonard's Girls' School and I see faces pressed against the windows. One girl, who I can tell is older than me and has long brown curly hair, sees me looking and waves. I wave back and watch her face as the bus carries her away. I turn off Sandling Road onto the long driveway down to the old manor house that is the main building of Brockhill, and enter the maelstrom of the playground, where hundreds of boys are shouting, running and fighting. It is terrifying. My new briefcase gets snatched out of my hand and thrown to another boy who opens it up and tips out the contents.

The school is so big and there is so much to remember just to find my way around. Our form room is a Portakabin and next door is another that houses a group of rough-looking boys with a year to fill as they are not taking exams, but are not allowed to leave school until they are sixteen. They are bored and glower at us through the windows. It feels as though there is menace and danger around every corner. At lunchtime I find a place of safety on a staircase overlooking the playground. From here are tantalising glimpses of fields and woodland that surround the school where everything is calm. Another first-year boy leans next to me on the rail and asks what pop groups I like. I say I don't really like any, which seems to confuse him, so we stand next to each other in silence. Then he gestures toward the swarm below. 'Lot of cunts here,' he says and I agree. When I get home, Dad asks me what my fellow pupils are like. I tell him they are 'a lot of cunts'. Dad is absolutely furious and says he thought this would happen if I went to a secondary modern.

When it is time for school assembly, hundreds of boys file into the big hall and slump down in rows, first-years at the front, sixth-formers at the back, ties done up in big knots, top buttons undone.

'Sit up straight,' says Mr Walton in a thick Yorkshire accent. He is the teacher in charge of technical drawing and has a large veined nose I see up close when he calls me to the front and holds my face in profile to say to the class I am a handsome boy. I find this disturbing but my classmates think it is funny. Mr Walton is leading assembly today. 'I am going to play you a record,' he tells us. 'It is a pop record and I am playing it because it has an important message you would do well to understand.' Then he gives us a stern warning. 'Just because it's pop music I don't want you clapping your hands and stamping your feet.' He puts the needle on the record and in the crackling that precedes the first note we all wonder what it could be. 'Stones,' whispers one boy. 'Beatles,' says another. 'T. Rex,' says a third. It is 'Happiness' by Ken Dodd. No one claps their hands and no one stamps their feet.

The music lessons are the one thing I really enjoy. The teacher, Mr Baulch, rewards our good behaviour by playing for us at the end. It is now Friday afternoon and sunlight streams through the windows of the classroom. I'm sitting three rows from the front and we are all excited as the weekend begins in ten minutes. Mr Baulch asks what we want to hear and we all shout for 'The Entertainer' by Scott Joplin, a tune that's popular because it is used in a film. Mr Baulch sits at the piano, adjusts his glasses, strokes his beard, flexes his fingers and begins to play. The ragtime tune bounces around the panelled walls of the classroom and fills us up with music. Sitting in my seat that afternoon, with 'The Entertainer' swirling about me, I learn to dance on the inside, to sit still and not betray any emotion while the music makes me feel hopeful, happy and euphoric. When the piece ends we applaud and cheer. Mr Baulch stands up and gives a theatrical bow. Then the bell sounds for the end of the day and we grab our bags and coats and rush out into the sunshine, ragtime piano playing in our heads as we run up the drive towards home.

Blackbird, 2015

My Martin acoustic guitar had been a companion for the last eighteen years and survived successive house moves in the countryside, the attention of two young children, a divorce and a new life back in Bristol. I bought it the day before my daughter Poppy was born. Then, I was working as a producer for BBC Radio 4 in Bristol but had a parallel career as a voiceover artist. While no one has ever said I have a lovely singing voice, my speaking voice has been complimented over the years and after a lucky break I started recording voiceovers for television and radio adverts. Sometimes this was extremely lucrative. A couple of weeks previously I had sat in a darkened recording studio and said 'SWEB. Working hard to get it right.' These seven words – a television advert for South Western Electricity Board – bought me a Martin acoustic guitar from a little shop up the road from the maternity hospital. I thought that buying an expensive guitar would keep my troubadour fantasy alive in the years to come when the focus of attention would be diverted elsewhere.

Like a lot of guitarists, I had believed that somewhere

out there was *the one*, the instrument that would make all the difference, and if only I could find *the one* my playing would magically transform as the guitar itself would make me really good. I had noticed how, when I visited a music shop, I would often see a man on a stool in the corner, picking the riff from 'Blackbird' by the Beatles on an expensive acoustic guitar, stroking the neck with the tenderness of a lover who hoped he had found *the one*. I thought I could see lost dreams in his eyes and carried on searching. Then, when it seemed as if time was running out, I tried the Martin. CF Martin & Company have a factory in Nazareth, Pennsylvania that makes expensive hand-crafted guitars, revered by players around the world. Sitting on a chair in the shop I strummed a few chords and picked a few tunes. 'Sounding sweet,' said the young salesman, who seemed to know what he was talking about, with his long hair tied into a ponytail, a faded T-shirt and eager smile. I knew in my heart this was not *the one*, but it was very nice and I had won the approval of the guitar man in the shop. Seduced by his flattery and knowing the Martin brand would impress other musicians, I said I would have it. I hoped we might learn to love each other. Over the years we indeed became very close, and I began to believe that this particular guitar was central to achieving my troubadour dreams. And now here it is, broken in my arms.

(What's So Funny 'Bout) Peace, Love and Understanding, 1973

It is now December and the shops in Canterbury are full of decorations. We have come to have Christmas lunch with my grandmother and her friend, Mrs Edwards. This is something we do every year and is a marker on the path that leads to Christmas itself, although this year I am not quite as excited as I have been before. In fact I am much more excited knowing I will be a teenager in exactly three months' time than by the thought of turkey and silly hats. As ever we arrive early. I no longer want to accompany Mum and Dad while they ponder over pillowcases and kitchen implements, so wander off alone, with the strict instruction to be back at the Elizabethan Tea Rooms at twelve-thirty. Walking up the High Street I see a display board mounted on an easel on the other side of the road. Around the display a group of hippies are collecting money in tins. Crossing the road to have a closer look I see a map of Canterbury on the board, on which is drawn a series of concentric circles, depicting the different levels of destruction an atom bomb would cause if it exploded in the middle of the city. There are also black-and-white photographs of a place in Japan where an atom bomb was dropped showing what it was like before and afterwards. Before, it could have been Canterbury and after there is nothing left. Most shocking are the pictures of people who were injured by the blast, the patterns on their clothes burned into their skin. I look up and imagine a bomb falling from the cold blue sky and exploding above the cathedral. Suddenly everything seems precarious. I cannot understand why everyone is not paying attention to the display. Most people are ignoring the hippies altogether and I watch an angry-looking man pull his wife out of the way when one of them tries to put a leaflet in her hand. I walk away up the road but cannot see the point of shopping when we could be blown up at any moment. I want to let the hippies know I am on their side so keep walking to and fro past the stand with ten pence in my hand, hoping that one of them will shake their tin in my direction. I have to walk past four times before a man with long straggly hair spots me. Before I put my money in his tin I want to show how much I agree with him by making the peace sign I recently learned from a friend. I raise my right hand, making a V with my fingers and say, 'Peace and love, man.' I try to speak with the laid-back drawl I have heard on the television, but as it comes out of my mouth I know it sounds like I am being rude. The hippie looks at me for a moment, shakes his head then moves away and I never get to put the money in his tin.

Because I have been walking up and down the road I am late for lunch with Grandma and Mrs Edwards and Mum is cross. When Christmas dinner is served by a waitress in Elizabethan costume, I am still thinking about the circles on the map of Canterbury and how everything is more frightening than it was this morning. After lunch Mrs Edwards gives me a transistor radio she doesn't want any more. It is not much bigger than the palm of my hand, made of thick, cream-coloured plastic, and protected by a brown leather case. She also hands me a single earpiece that plugs into the side, and says that I will be able to listen to it at night and Mum and Dad will never know.

I am still thinking about the atom bomb when I go to bed that evening. I plug the earpiece into the radio and turn the little wheel that scans the airwaves. I pass through Morse code, foreign voices and static until I come to Radio Caroline. Somewhere out in the dark North Sea is a ship called the *Mi Amigo* that is a pirate radio station, which means it is illegal. I lay in the warmth of stripy pyjamas and mustard-coloured sheets as a disc jockey plays records that sound as strange and confused as I feel. When Christmas comes I still get swept up by the excitement of it all, though when I leave a glass of sherry and a mince pie for Father Christmas, it is just to make Mum and Dad feel happy. I don't believe in Father Christmas any more.

Doctor! Doctor!, 2015

Four o'clock on a Saturday afternoon is not the best time to look for an instrument repairer, but such is my desperation that within a few minutes I locate a music shop that takes repairs and call them. The man I speak to sounds like a doctor calming a frightened patient, blended with a mechanic talking to someone who knows nothing about cars. He has seen all sorts in his time and it probably isn't terminal, he tells me, but I should bring the guitar in right away because he can only diagnose when he sees the damage. Half an hour later, as the dark afternoon becomes a winter evening, I walk from the cold street into the bright lights of the guitar shop, where perfect instruments hang on the walls. I grip my guitar case and hope it is not a coffin. The man looks at the damage and sucks air through his teeth. 'We can fix it,' he says. 'It'll take a couple of weeks and it won't be cheap.'

Tiger Feet, 1974

It is a freezing Thursday night in January and I have been at secondary school for just over a term. Come into our living room. It is looking a bit empty because the Christmas decorations have just been taken down. There is a big mound of coal burning in the fireplace and I am sitting cross-legged on the floor wearing polyester school trousers and a green V-neck jumper. Something else has changed too. I have become one of 15 million other people watching *Top of the Pops* on this cold night. Even though I don't like pop music I have started to watch this show every week. The programme gives me something to talk about at school but I still don't like the nonsense they sing about. 'If you can even call it singing,' says Mum. And up until now I have agreed with her.

My dad walks into the living room holding a tea towel and a wet plate. He does this from time to time when *Top of the Pops* is on so he can stand and watch and shake his head. At this very moment the group Mud come onto the screen. They are wearing bright suits and one of them is wearing a dress and large dangly earrings. 'Goodness gracious...' he says. '…Look at them… just look at them.' And that's when I decide to try out another new word I have heard being used at school.

I say, 'Dad, I think they're quite cool.'

Dad has a look on his face like I have suddenly started speaking in tongues.

'Cool?' he says. 'Did you just say the word *cool*? Wherever have you got that from?'

'It's what they are, Dad,' I say.

He splutters and points the tea towel at the screen. 'But they're not even playing… Look, they're just pretending.'

I watch my dad pad back into the kitchen in his slippers and brown cardigan, still shaking his head. And I look at Mud on the television dancing around in their bright suits, and singing about tiger feet that are neat. And not only do I believe in that moment that they *are* actually quite cool, but that it might also be quite cool to be one of Mud and to get to dance around on the television in a bright suit pretending to sing.

How Do Ya Fix a Broken Part, 2015

Two weeks later I call the man at the guitar shop in Bristol and he tells me the repair is going to take longer. He explains the luthier – the lovely antiquated name for the profession of the person repairing my Martin – is using a glue that will only set once the ambient temperature is above a certain point. Because the weather has turned cold the repair cannot begin. I call again when the weather is not so cold and am told the weather forecast must predict at least four consecutive warm days before anything can happen. I realise this could all take some time and decide to invest in another guitar.

Things have moved on and Sarah and I are now going out together. She lives in Cardiff, so I am spending more time in Wales. In the middle of the city is a big music shop called Cranes, a family-run store that is something of a local institution. Coming off the street I pause to look at expensive instruments locked in glass cases, before carrying on to a large room at the back, where cheaper guitars are displayed on floor stands, hung from walls and suspended from the high ceiling. I want something small enough to take on road trips and I don't have much money. The salesman – friendly, long hair, T-shirt, permanently rushing around – winces appropriately when I describe the moment of weightlessness as the Martin fell through the air. He suggests I try a parlour guitar and sets me up in a demonstration room.

One of the problems with trying out a guitar in a music shop is sharing space with other buyers who are picking, strumming and riffing at the same time. I can't hear myself above the cacophony, begin to believe I am the worst player in the room, and then start to play badly. But in the privacy of the demonstration room I play without inhibition and sing as well. I am halfway through 'Boulder to Birmingham' when the door opens and the salesman comes in. I stop immediately but he tells me to carry on, so I do and finish the song.

'Sounding good,' he says. 'Are you gigging at the moment?'

No sweeter words could have been spoken than those last six. Although I know this man's job is to sell guitars, I am flattered by how genuine the question seems to be. I start to talk and when I do I hear myself laying out a whole secret plan that had been forming in my head.

'I haven't sung a song on stage for more than thirty years,' I say. 'But I'm going to go out on tour and play… well… everywhere.' As I speak my troubadour dream comes alive again and I see myself out on the road, travelling from town to town with this little guitar in my hand. I am still talking as I hand over the money, barely letting the salesman get a word in edgeways. But before I leave he manages to ask one more question.

'Why did you stop singing?'

Queen Bitch, 1975

I keep my admiration for Mud secret from everybody, partly because I cannot understand why I suddenly like them so much. The band have another hit in the charts called 'The Cat Crept In' and I like that too. One day I casually mention all this to my French teacher, Mr Smith – who is young and seems to be pretty cool himself – but he shakes his head and says something rude, so I keep quiet about my change of mind.

'What do you want to be when you grow up?' This question is asked whenever I meet aunts, uncles or friends of my parents. I used to say I wanted to be an astronaut, which would make the adults laugh because I am so afraid of heights. Sometimes I say I would like to be a farmer and no one laughs at that. There is a farm at our school and I have been enjoying our rural science lessons in the classroom that looks over the cowshed. Some of my new friends already know what they want to be. Colin will be an artist and Fred is going to be a musician. Fred is tall and thin with long straight hair that hangs from a centre parting to either side of his face. After school we walk home together with another friend called Andy. Mum has just started a new job as a secretary at the local girls' school and doesn't get home until half past four. Because I don't like letting myself into an empty house, I keep my friends talking by the lamppost down the road until she comes past in the Morris Traveller. What we are going to be when we grow up is often discussed. Fred tells us how he is learning to play the piano and guitar and wants to be in a group. I respond by repeating what Mum and Dad say when they see a pop group on television. 'It's all very well having long hair and making a racket for a living when you're young,' I mimic. 'But what are you going to do when it all stops? What then? What are you going to do when you want to buy a house and have a baby? What then?'

Fred nods his head like someone wise beyond his years. 'Yes, I know,' he says. 'But I still want to do it.'

Our lamppost conversations continue as winter turns to spring. Fred just nods when I say what a dreadful world pop music is and almost no one ever *makes it*. As I understand – again from Mum and Dad – pop musicians are very poor until they *make it*, when they are propelled onto television and have loads of money they do not know how to spend properly. The act of making it seems to be a mysterious thing and different from most jobs where you work hard and get promotion. There seems to be no middle ground; either you *make it* or you don't. Fred has a cousin in a group and they have a record coming out which sounds as if they've *made it*, but Fred says they are not famous yet as people have to buy the record first.

Also, Mum and Dad talk about how pop musicians are *on drugs*, which sounds like a terrible thing, but Fred says not all of them are. As time passes I still repeat what Mum and Dad are saying but start to believe it less and less. Then one day Fred brings a guitar into school and plays it in front of me and I sit a couple of feet away watching his fingers move across the strings as he strums bits of songs by groups I have never heard before. Boys cluster and watch, even those who are normally more interested in fighting. Someone asks if Fred can play 'Smoke on the Water' by Deep Purple and he plays something that makes the boys shake their heads in time with the music.

'Mud? You're not listening to Mud, are you?' That is what Fred says when I eventually tell him. I say that I think they're quite a good *pop group*. 'They're not,' he says. 'They're really not. And don't call them a pop group like that. It's not cool.' I try to hide my surprise at what Fred has just told me. I imagined all pop music was cool, so it is very confusing to discover some is and some isn't. 'Mud are crap,' he tells me. 'Like most of the other stuff in the charts.'

I want to know what I should be listening to and Fred gives me a big, long list. King Crimson; Led Zeppelin; Yes; Genesis; Crosby, Stills, Nash & Young; Pink Floyd; Emerson, Lake & Palmer; David Bowie… The list goes on and on. It turns out there are divisions, subdivisions and rules about what you can and can't like that are as complicated and confusing as football. And football is completely baffling. At school yesterday I was laughed at by the whole class when I said I preferred Tottenham to Hotspur. As I said goodbye to my teachers at primary school I thought I knew everything, but now I am beginning to realise I know nothing at all.

Fred picks up a record from the top of a pile and shows me the sleeve, on which there is a picture of David Bowie looking upward with his hand against his head. The record is called *Hunky Dory*. When I look closely at the picture, Bowie has long hair like a girl, and from the face I can't tell whether it is a man or a woman I am looking at. I keep my confusion to myself as Fred takes the disc from the sleeve. 'Listen to this,' he says, dropping the needle down on a track near the end of side two. '"Queen Bitch",' he tells me, before the song begins. First of all there is an acoustic guitar, then over the top comes an electric guitar out of the left speaker. 'Mick Ronson,' shouts Fred over the music. Then another electric guitar comes out of the right speaker. The sound is distorted and exciting and it feels like I am being shaken by the shoulders and told to wake up.

Movin' On Up, 2015

I am not ready to admit it to a stranger in a shop, or even to travel the back roads in my mind and confront the reasons why it began, but I suffer from stage fright. When I sing in my kitchen I am fine and when I sing on a recording I can always start again, but even thinking about an audience in front of me my hands start to sweat and my breathing becomes erratic. I forget the words and, worst of all, sing out of tune. This is strange because I can speak freely in front of groups of students and deliver lectures without notes. But then, I reason, I can um and er as much as I want, or take a divergent path and find my way back again. None of these freedoms is available when singing. Singing is a precision activity, and the success of a live song depends on words delivered as musical notes in the right order, accompanied by another set of notes generated by two hands working the guitar.

One evening I meet some friends in a bar on a converted barge in Bristol. Among them is Jane Harbour, the violin player and main composer in Spiro, a band who play instrumental music, blending original and traditional melodies with minimalism, to make something new and exciting. I have seen Spiro play often and am always impressed by the exuberance of their performances. With her red hair and long, swirling dresses, Jane is a striking presence. Moving to the rhythm of the music and striding about the stage, she is the very definition of a confident performer, even when playing the most complex pieces. I ask where this self-assurance comes from.

'Practice,' says Jane. 'I practise until I know the piece so well that when I step on stage, muscle memory takes over.'

I used to keep the guitar in my kitchen and play while pretending to do other things. I hadn't thought of it as practice, just something I did. Now I start to consciously practise every day, breaking songs down and putting them back together again, identifying places where I make mistakes and working on those sections. I hope that when the time comes I will have enough muscle memory to carry me through. I sing to Sarah when she comes to see me, with the caveat that if it gets too much she will tell me to shut up. She never does and so I have an audience of one.

Then, it is a chilly night in April and I am back on the Isles of Scilly running a writing course at Carnwethers, the very place where Patrick and Lisa had their farewell party two years before. We have just finished the last session when one of the students asks if I would end the evening by singing songs. This time I do not make an excuse. Clutching a borrowed acoustic guitar and a bottle of wine, I lead a small group out to a cold, clear night to perch on sunbeds around the covered-up swimming pool. So, there we all are, wrapped up against the cold under a sky full of stars. The smokers roll cigarettes, someone pours wine into glasses and the conversation stills. Then, I begin to sing. I know as I play it is not perfect but no one is listening for mistakes, they are enjoying the night. One of the gang asks me to sing 'Fairytale of New York' over and over again, which I do until the others get fed up, at which point I put down the guitar. Then we walk to the beach and lie on white sand, looking up at the stars. Many years ago, I interviewed Bob Geldof for a radio programme, where he described the ecstasy of being slightly drunk after a gig in Australia, lying on the bonnet of a car and looking up at the night sky. He was in his early forties and still doing it, still living the dream. I had just played a few songs by a covered-up swimming pool, but lying here on the sands of Pelistry beach I knew exactly what he meant.

Wild Thing, 1975

I am sitting in Fred's house on the seafront, which is always full of brothers and sisters and music. I look out through the window to the English Channel that is flat and grey and seems to go on for ever. A fishing boat moves slowly over the water like it can't be bothered. I have come here today because Fred is going to give me a guitar lesson. He picks up his acoustic guitar and places his long, thin fingers on the fretboard to show me the chord of E. When I try to copy him it is almost impossible, but Fred moves my fingers into position and tells me to strum with my right hand. When I do it sounds something like a chord, though by the time I try again my fingers have moved, deadening the strings. Fred rearranges his fingers to show me the chord of A, which is really hard too. Finally Fred shows me the chord of B. This one, he says, is a bar chord, and it will be a while before I have the strength in my fingers to play it. He tells me to keep practising every day and if I do, then it will come. I watch him carefully. He knows so much about music already. Music seems to flow through him. It doesn't appear to take any effort.

Music is becoming important because it says something beyond words. Music floods my senses with so much feeling. And the guitar seems to be a doorway into the secret world of songs. If I could be the one to actually make those songs come alive, imagine how much more intense those feelings would be. Then Fred gives me the most important piece of information in the whole lesson. Put these three chords together, he says, and you can play loads of songs. He demonstrates with the opening chords of the song 'Wild Thing'. 'Why don't you sing it?' he says.

A shudder like an electric charge goes through my whole body. I really, really want to be able to sing out loud in front of other people. Once it was something so easy but since I started at secondary school everything has changed. It's like the world has been divided into the people with good voices and everyone else. And I'm everyone else. But here is a song I can just roar. Fred gives me a nod, which is a sign to open my mouth and begin.

I've been noticing things recently. I've been noticing how there are net curtains everywhere and everyone is hiding behind them peering out. As I belt out the words it feels like I'm tearing down the net curtains and not hiding any more.

I roar the second line, and it is so not like singing in church on a Sunday or in school assembly.

The line ends with the word *groovy*, and it feels so good to bark it out, because nothing in my world is groovy. Not the flat calm English Channel in front of me, not the High

Street, not the church on the hill and not me. But just singing it in a song makes me feel a bit more groovy than I did before.

Oh My Sweet Carolina, 2015

It is a still night in summer when Sarah and I sit on a bench in the dark. In the distance a few people are clustered around a firebowl, faces illuminated by flickering flames, woodsmoke drifting on a light sea breeze. On our faces we feel the sun that has been shining all day and between the picked notes of my guitar, I hear waves breaking on the beach far below. I have joined Sarah on a family holiday in West Wales. After months in the kitchen, it feels like liberation to be playing in the open air again, a wall behind me supporting the sound, carrying it towards the dark ocean. Someone says it is nice to hear me sing so I carry on. I can tell from the talking and laughter that none of the firebowl crowd is actually listening, so making background music is a stealthy way of normalising performance for me.

Sometimes it feels good to strum the guitar using a plectrum and sometimes to pick with the fingers themselves. Strumming is louder and generates a percussive energy, but the atmosphere this evening demands quieter music, so I pick my way through my small repertoire of folk and Americana songs. Among them is a gentle ballad by American songwriter Ryan Adams, called 'Oh My Sweet Carolina'; a story of somebody lost and far from home. I think of the night in Byron Bay twenty years ago when I was desperate to sing; if I could have sung anything then it would have been this.

Later I talk to a heavily bearded local in the hotel bar. He asks if I am hoping to be *spotted*. I say that I am too old to be *spotted*, which gets a laugh, perhaps too much of a laugh, but I think about it afterwards and it takes me back to a time when being *spotted* seemed the only way to *make it*. This belief in a sort of divine intervention is a powerful myth and lives on to this day in shows like *X Factor* and *The Voice*, where judges line up like gods to bestow wisdom and largesse on the chosen ones. There was a time when I did hope that would happen to me, but not any more. Honestly.

The conversation in the bar makes me think about the bands on the circuit in Kent. I remember so many musicians saying they were on the verge of something bigger, reporting a chance meeting with someone who knew someone who was going to make all the difference. Then a month or so later I would see them again and the transformation had not happened. I start to think about a band called Naughty Thoughts I used to follow around Kent and who seemed most likely to break out from their backwater into the mainstream. They played tuneful songs with punky energy and their cover of the Small Faces song 'All or Nothing' was a record I nearly wore out. When I left home I lost interest in Naughty

Thoughts and imagined they gave up and got proper jobs along with everyone else. So it is a pleasant surprise to discover, via an internet search, that they went from playing tiny basements in Folkestone to having a number-one hit in Germany. I even find a recording on YouTube and see their familiar faces under dyed blond mullet haircuts. Underneath, someone has written a derogatory comment about the song, to which someone else – a member of the band I presume – has responded: '375k, a new house and a brand-new car. Who's laughing now... TWAT.'

A few days later we take the guitar to a shelter on a path that overlooks the bay. I start to sing 'The Shoals of Herring' – a song by Ewan MacColl – as I look through fine rain to where the cliffs disappear into mist. The tide is high and the waves are breaking at the entrance of the bay, sending a thin spread of foamy water across the beach. A man, wrapped up in a cagoule, walks past with a small dog on a long lead. The dog stops and looks at me while the man walks on. When he reaches the length of the lead the man stops too, just out of sight, as the dog carries on watching. At the end of the song, the lead is given a yank and the dog trots away. Next day I am walking on another cliff path when I see the man and the dog again. When I bend to stroke the dog, the man tells me he stood just out of sight because he didn't want to disturb me, but had enjoyed my singing and wanted to stay for longer. If you are a seasoned performer then you might wonder why I have devoted a paragraph to a compliment from a stranger on a footpath. If you are as terrified as I was you will understand. At some point I would have to move on from stealth gigs in clifftop shelters and walk on to a stage. The endorsement of an unknown man on a footpath was a friendly push towards the stage lights.

Stardust, 1975

'What on earth have you got on your feet?' I am wearing the brown platform shoes I have just persuaded Mum to buy in the sale at Freeman, Hardy and Willis in the High Street, and Dad has come home from work to find me tottering up and down the hall.

'All my friends have got them,' I say, stroking the fine layer of downy hair on my upper lip and rubbing the spot on my face. 'They're really cool.' I cannot believe Mum agreed to buy them, although she seemed to regret the decision immediately.

'I don't know what people are going to think when they see you,' she says.

Dad tries to be funny. 'The air must be really thin up there. It's a wonder you can breathe.'

I roll my eyes and shake my head. 'I don't care what people think.'

And with that I march out of the front door, slamming it behind me. I am a full inch and a half higher and stop in the drive to adjust to the strange feeling of being tall. Look at me now, clip-clopping down the avenue, trousers flapping at my ankles, imagining the tuts of disapproval from behind the net curtains of Hythe. Actually, no one is looking.

Now it is half term and I am standing outside the Mecca cinema at the end of the High Street with Fred and Andy. We are here to see a film called *Stardust* with David Essex that has a double A rating, meaning you have to be over fourteen to get in. I am hoping the extra height from the platform soles will do the trick. We hang around for as long as possible, putting off the encounter with the lady in the box office. My mouth is dry and it is not until the matinee is about to start that we stride into the lobby. The cashier is chewing gum and talking to another woman, so doesn't even look at me as I hand over my forty-five pence and walk inside. An usher with a torch shows us to our places near the front and I turn to look at the rows of empty seats behind us. Then the lights go down, the curtains part and the adverts begin.

The singer David Essex has already caused hilarity with Mum and Dad because he sings in a cockney accent, which is further evidence of the uncouthness of pop music. The film is about a pop group whose rise to fame unfolds on the vast screen right in front of us. Towards the end is a scene in a recording studio late at night. Girls are giggling in the semi-darkness, then suddenly we see them without any clothes on. One of the band pours what looks to me like sherry over a girl's breasts. I can't breathe and I find myself thinking of the bottle of amontillado tucked away in the drinks cabinet at home. I cannot look at Andy or Fred. I feel as though I should look away, but I can't. I see a girl's breast glistening with golden liquid. Then suddenly the image of my dad pouring a small glass of sherry for my mum on Christmas Day pops into my head.

When the film is over we walk into twilight. For a while no one speaks. My shoes clip-clop up the High Street, past Griggs the fishmonger, Eakins the chemist and Eldridges the draper. Nothing looks quite the same any more. We are all thinking the same thing but Andy says it first.

'Shall we get a band together?'

I remember the dark studio and the sherry. 'Do you think we could do it?' I reply.

Andy thinks for a moment. 'I could learn the drums,' he says. I start to hear the roar of a mighty crowd. 'What about you, Fred?' says Andy.

'I think you two need to learn to play first,' he says, which is not the same as yes but isn't no either.

Back at home I take off my platform shoes in the hall, carry them upstairs and put them on again. Then I get my nylon-strung acoustic guitar and stand in front of the full-length mirror on the landing. I see my big nose and black curly hair brushed straight and given a side parting by my mum. I wonder if I will ever look like a rock star.

These Streets, 2015

I lose touch with Fred when I move away from Hythe. Andy, who went away and came back again, thinks he went to live in New York. I have not seen Fred for over thirty years but as I gear up to perform again I want to know what happened to him, the most likely of us all to become a professional musician. If he had *made it*, I probably would have known. I really hope he is still out there playing somewhere. At first I can't find a trace, until deeper searching reveals he has extended his surname from simply Fred Davies to Fred Gregory Davies, and is not in New York at all, but married and living near Brighton with two boys. He is also, I discover, actively engaged in music, playing guitar and mandolin in a band called Hatful of Rain, who have released records and played live on the Bob Harris show on BBC Radio 2. I find the video for 'These Streets', a really catchy song, and there is Fred miming the guitar and riding on a bicycle, three decades on and looking just as I hoped he would. There is the same haircut, the centre parting and long hair on either side. Looking for live dates I discover Hatful of Rain are appearing in Cardiff in a few weeks' time.

Dempseys is an Irish pub on Castle Street in the centre of town with an iconic music venue above the bar. There is a banner in the window with a quote from the American jazz saxophonist Charlie Parker: 'If you don't live it, it won't come out of your horn.' I pay £12 and go upstairs, see Fred straight away and pause for a moment, taking in the familiar shape of my old friend. Some of us have expanded since our early twenties, but Fred is suitably lean, standing near a bay window near the low stage and gazing out at the floodlit walls of Cardiff Castle. I say hello and he responds in the same way I do when somebody thinks they know me and I am not quite sure who they are. Then his eyes widen. 'Paul,' he says. 'It's Paul.' And rests a hand on my shoulder. I buy him a drink and we sit down and talk.

Hatful of Rain play tuneful American-influenced folk music on double bass, violin, banjo and acoustic guitar, with layered vocal harmonies. This night in Cardiff they cluster around a single microphone, swapping instruments between songs and performing with delicate virtuosity. When I last saw Fred he played the guitar and a little piano. Now, here he is riffing on the mandolin, playing slide guitar as well as banjo and double bass. It makes me think about natural musical ability. In his book *Musicophilia: Tales of Music and the Brain*, the neurologist Oliver Sacks writes, 'What one calls musicality comprises a great range of skills and receptivities, from the most elementary perception of pitch and tempo to the highest aspects of musical intelligence and sensibility.'

Watching him now, I remember how effortless Fred made it seem to be and how hard I have to work to make anything sound good.

There are not many people in the audience to begin with, though it gets busier as the evening progresses. Afterwards we sit down together again and Fred tells me what has happened in the last thirty years. He never stopped playing and had familiar stories of near misses with the big time. When he got married and moved to Brighton, Fred realised he needed a steady source of income to subsidise his passion for music and so retrained as a carpenter. Now he makes bespoke wooden furniture and plays in several bands. 'I feel like I should apologise,' he says. 'When I taught you to play the guitar I completely ignored the fact you were left-handed.' I tell him not to worry. No one will ever write about me in a guitar magazine but I play well enough to get by. I tell him that although we had lost touch, he had never gone away, so when I had a son and we needed a name, it is no coincidence that Fred came to the surface.

Caroline, 1975

Andy's mum and dad run Whitegates old people's home in the middle of Hythe. And that is where we are now, behind the net curtains in the living room of the flat where they live, onsite. I am holding my acoustic guitar and Andy has a pair of drumsticks and sits in front of a bucket turned upside down. We don't have an actual drum yet. We are trying to play a song I have written about a teacher at school. It is called 'The Diddyman Blues' but I can't always change chords quickly enough, so we drift out of time with each other. My left hand seems to work fine on the fretboard, but my right is much harder to control. Picking seems impossible so Fred has suggested I concentrate on strumming, bringing my hand up and down with even strokes and brushing a plastic plectrum against the strings. What I am hearing in my head is not the choppy, uneven sound that comes from the guitar. Sometimes I see a guitarist on television with head back, eyes shut and fingers that seem to fly across the fretboard. It looks so effortless. Whenever I am alone in my bedroom I practise my chords and the little riffs taught to me by Fred, wondering how anyone can get to be that good, when my improvement is so slow.

Mum and Dad go to Folkestone once a week to do their shopping in a newly opened supermarket. I stay behind. The first time they leave me alone I hear something creaking and think a robber has broken into the house. I imagine him creeping around downstairs and working his way towards me. I pick up the Bible and stand on the landing at the top of the stairs proclaiming a bloodthirsty section of the Old Testament until the noises stop. As time goes on I start to realise these absences are opportunities. Their shopping trips are always on a Thursday evening and coincide with *Top of the Pops*. Even though none of us likes music in the charts we all still watch it, and with Mum and Dad out of the way I can enjoy the fleshy dance routines of Pan's People without having to pretend I am not interested.

Dad has taken up pipe smoking and I think it is something I would like to try. I take the pipe, fill it with tobacco and go into the sideway with a box of matches. When I empty the pipe afterwards I am amazed that the tobacco is mostly intact. One of the mysteries of smoking, I imagine. A month or so later I discover the tobacco has never been alight and what I had thought was smoke is just cloud breath. Then there is the drinks cupboard. In the living room are bottles of sherry, gin, whisky, Cinzano and a few strangely coloured liqueurs. At school, boys are talking about the amazing effects of drunkenness and how it makes music sound better.

So another part of my Thursday routine is to fill half a liqueur glass and sip at it slowly while watching *Top of the Pops*. Nothing much seems to happen and they taste pretty horrible. Every time I refill the bottles with water and am never discovered.

Then it is a Friday evening in October and there is a disco in Cheriton, five miles from Hythe. Andy's father drives us there and my dad will come and pick us up when it finishes at ten o'clock sharp. At home I get ready by shaving off the hairs on my lip, brushing my curly hair until it becomes a sort of dome, then slap on Brut 33 aftershave all over my body. I put on a printed shirt, Birmingham baggy trousers and my platform shoes. As we walk into the church hall a disco song is playing, lights are flashing and the DJ – who has big white headphones over a balding head and wears a brightly coloured Hawaiian shirt – is hunched over his console lining up the next record. Groups of boys and girls are clustered on each side of the hall, pretending not to look while sizing each other up. The music is from the charts, so we stand to one side and look bored, secretly wishing we were less awkward. I am envious of the lithe boys, fluent on the dance floor, smiling at the girls who are dancing too. The DJ announces each song by putting on a strange accent, pretending he is on the radio, and Andy and I grimace at each other as records by the Stylistics, the Chi-Lites and KC and the Sunshine Band fill the hall with bright disco music and dances copied from *Top of the Pops*. Our friend Chris has asked the DJ for a request and as time goes on we become impatient, waiting to hear the introduction to the one song we like. Finally, it happens. First the distorted rock and roll guitar riff, then another guitar, then the DJ shouts over the top in his made-up accent: 'It's time to rock and roll. It's time for Status Quo. It's time… for… sweet… "Caroline"!' He tries to rhyme *time* with *Caroline*, which sounds terrible, and to stop speaking when the drums and bass come in, which he can only do by extending the last syllable of Caroline so it comes out as *Caroliiiiiiiiiiiiiiiiiine*. Then he stands back from his record decks, puts his hands in his pockets, makes V shapes with his arms and does the Status Quo dance all on his own, legs firmly planted on the wooden floorboards, thrusting left and right in time with the music.

At the end of the evening the dance floor clears when the DJ puts on a slow record and ranks of girls and boys line up on either side of the hall. The confident boys stride out across the floorboards to pluck out willing girls, leading them to the middle, embracing them and swaying slowly to the music. I look across the divide at the faces of the girls, hoping for a signal that an invitation to dance might be accepted, so the long walk across the dance floor would not end with a humiliating shake of their head. But the girls are not looking any more; they have turned inward and are talking to their friends. By now boys have started kissing girls, mouths locked together as Leo Sayer sings 'When I Need You' and the lights flash green, orange and red. I catch the eye of a girl called

Debbie on the other side and she looks away, but right before she does I think she smiles. I have a moment to read her smile, to decide if it is an invitation. I have never had a proper conversation with Debbie, but we have exchanged a few furtive looks. She is blonde, taller than me and as my mum might say, well developed. I decide to take the risk and feel my heart pounding beneath my printed shirt and a film of sweat forming on my hands as I weave through the snoggers. Debbie sees me coming and turns into her group of friends. I tap her shoulder and ask – trying to sound as if I don't care – whether she would like a dance. Debbie nods and moves away from her friends, following me to the middle of the dance floor where we wrap our arms around each other. As I sway to the music I seek the best place for my hands on her back, sensing her breasts below my face and trying not to dip my chin into her cleavage. Then I turn my face upwards as Debbie turns hers down. We rub our cheeks together before I take a chance and risk an exploratory peck on the side of her face. When the slow dance ends our eyes are shut and our mouths clamped together. Then the DJ says goodnight and bright strip lights are turned on, to reveal parents in anoraks standing awkwardly, just inside the door.

Meanwhile, Andy carries on bashing the buckets and I carry on with the guitar. My chord changes get quicker and we find a name for our band. We are called the Entangled Network. Andy discovers it is possible for the N to be joined to the bottom of the E and for our name to be abbreviated to a logo, EN. I find some wet concrete in a side road off the High Street and trace EN with my fingers, so it sets and stays there for years. I draw EN on my leather briefcase and we seem to be a band even before we know any songs.

Radio Radio, 2015

I carry on performing alone in my kitchen and fantasising about being on the road with a guitar and a headful of songs. I even tell people about my plans, but if anyone asks when they can come and see me, I say next year, because next year sounds far enough away not to worry about. My guitar-playing skills are tested when a radio play of mine – for which I also write the music – is recorded at a studio in Brighton. In the past I would have sat at home crafting the sound on my computer, recording retake after retake, stitching it all together and handing over a tape to the sound engineer. This time I will perform live in the studio, so travel to Brighton with two guitars, a long coat and a hat. The singing will be done by actors but I will play the guitar. For the first time in my life I have also let my hair grow long and have a beard. Mum tells me I look old but as I stagger up the London Road with my guitar cases I meet Celia, my producer, on her way to get coffee. 'God, you look like such a muso,' she says, which makes me feel quietly confident about the task ahead.

The play includes a reconstruction of a song sung at

a performance in a church. Celia decides the recording would be better if it really was a performance, so gathers the cast at one end of the studio, faced by myself and the two singing actors. As we wait for the green light I look at the accomplished performers around me, including a star of West End musicals and the singer from a very good band. It would be easy to feel intimidated, but in the weeks leading up to the session I have practised my part over and over again, so when the light flashes and I take a deep breath and play, my fingers do what they are supposed to and the singers wrap themselves around the sound of the guitar.

Eight Miles High, 1976

Because my friend Colin has older brothers, he gets to do things earlier than the rest of us and has already tried smoking cannabis. He tells us about all the things you have to do to roll a joint: a complex process involving resin, tobacco, cigarette papers and a bit of cardboard called a roach. He explains how you hold your breath after taking a lungful of smoke, how this makes you high and the world seems completely different. Best of all is that music sounds amazing. I would like to try a joint myself and Colin has said he will see what he can do. He has been lending me records I have been playing on the radiogram, bringing strange sounds into our living room. Because of the odd noises, combined with me being thirteen and stories in the papers about rock music and addiction, Mum starts to worry that I will go *on drugs*. According to Mum, you are either *on drugs* or you are not. And when you are *on drugs* that is the end of everything.

One day I am home with Mum who is ironing in the kitchen with the door into the hall wide open. There is a knock on the front door and I open it to find Colin on the step, unannounced.

'Do you want to come down the allotments for some blow, man?' he asks. I freeze and stare at his face. I hear the sound of the iron on the board in the kitchen. I continue to stare and Colin looks confused.

'Not now, no, I can't,' I say and Colin shrugs, turns around and heads off alone. I go back into the kitchen and scan Mum's face for clues. She has incredible hearing and knows when a drawer is being opened in my room, or worse, the sound of tissues being removed from a box. She had indeed heard every word and asks what Colin meant. I say it is just slang for a chat and go back upstairs, looking down the road from the window on the landing to watch Colin disappearing into a narrow path that leads to the allotments.

After school one day I go to Colin's home at the bottom of the big hill in Hythe. Colin has his own door key and lets himself in to an empty house. The house is empty because his dad died before we began at secondary school and his mum goes out to work. His brothers and sisters are out too so we are there alone. I am hoping Colin will suggest rolling a joint, but he tells me he hasn't got any at the moment and instead goes into a little room off the kitchen and comes out with a biscuit tin in which there are a few slices of toast he made before school this morning. We take those into his living room where the record player is kept. The band Genesis has just released a new album called *A Trick of the Tail* and one of

Colin's brothers bought it as soon as it came out. Colin tells me they used to have a singer called Peter Gabriel but he left the group and their drummer has become the new singer. We listen to the whole record, one side after another, and I wonder what it all *means*. When we study poems at school, or look at pieces of modern art, we are always looking for the *meaning*. I have learned that the words might say one thing, but the *meaning* is something else. So as I listen to each of the songs on *A Trick of the Tail*, I try to join them all together in the hope that some sort of story will reveal itself and the *meaning* will become clear. When that doesn't happen, I decide that either I am not looking hard enough or I am not yet old enough to understand. Of course I do not say any of this to Colin who nods his head every now and then as though he knows exactly what everything *means*.

Wessex Boy, 2015

Most of what I have learned so far are folk songs and I believe I'm on the way to becoming the sort of folk singer who will play sitting down and sing through his beard. Then, one night in November I go to see Frank Turner, whom I once saw play a storming late-afternoon set at a festival in Cornwall. He is a folk singer too, albeit with a jet pack attached to his acoustic guitar. He has toured relentlessly, selling out Wembley Arena and playing at the opening ceremony of the Olympics in 2012. Frank Turner inspires a fierce devotion in his fans so his weekend performances at the Colston Hall in Bristol were sold out months before, but late on Sunday afternoon I spot a ticket for the last show online. I head over to a house on a hill near the freight terminal at Avonmouth and hand twenty-five pounds to a young mum who had been let down by her babysitter. Then, with a pint of beer in my hand, I walk into the hall to spot an old friend standing near the front with his son and daughter, who just happens to be one of my daughter's best friends. Looking up at the seats on the balcony I see the mum of a girl who had been in my daughter's class at school. I think how unlikely it would have been for my dad to ever come with me to a show like this when I was in my late teens, when our taste in music was what set us apart, rather than brought us together. There are more men than women and they are mostly, but not exclusively, younger than me. Many are wearing well-worn T-shirts emblazoned with the artwork of one of Frank's albums, or dates of a previous tour.

I enjoy the two support acts and hold my position near the front as the audience start swarming into the mosh pit until we are a tightly packed crush. As the lights dim there is a great roar as Frank and his band stroll onto the stage. He wears skinny black jeans and a close-fitting white shirt, sleeves rolled up to show tattoos on his forearms and fingers, and has a wiry energy that kicks in as soon as the band begin to play. Between verses and in instrumental interludes, Frank bounces around the stage. Most of the audience know every word of every song and bounce around too, so the effect is like trying to stand still in a rough sea. The enthusiasm is so infectious I start bouncing too, self-consciously at first and then with abandon, though I can't keep up the bouncing and stop to watch every now and then, static in the surging crowd. What Frank Turner does is channel the incredible energy generated by nearly two thousand excited people to build a tangible sense of community in the hall and he does this with complete and utter commitment to the performance. There is no pretence at being the cool, aloof rock star; he feels like one of us, our mate up there on the stage. As Frank Turner writes in his gig diary, *The Road Beneath My Feet*, 'I'm always more interested in music when it breaks out of the mould and becomes a dialogue, an interaction, rather than just a lecture from "artist" to punter.'

When the show is over I walk into the night air soaking wet and thinking how wonderful it has been to be part of it all for a couple of hours. Here I am, a middle-aged man living on his own, but just for a short while I have been part of something bigger than me, bigger than us all. This, I remember, is what rock and roll can do and a moment of feeling like this makes everything worthwhile. It also makes me want to go out and play.

I unlock my bike outside the Colston Hall and cycle under the Suspension Bridge towards home, pedalling along the cycle path that runs by the dark river in the Avon Gorge. My ears are ringing and Frank Turner's songs are alive in my head. Go out and do it, he seems to be saying; don't let your life go past with your ambitions unrealised; don't let it all rush by and end up regretting what you haven't done.

In the Region of the Summer Stars, 1976

One day Colin comes to school with some amazing news: he is going to London with an older brother to see Elton John play at Earl's Court. I am intrigued and jealous all at once. When I tell Mum she shakes her head and says she remembers when it was safe to walk around London at night. So it is a surprise when Colin comes to school unharmed the day after the concert, full of excitement and telling the story of the night before. Earl's Court was as big as an aircraft hangar and packed with thousands of people; Elton John and his band were amazing; the music was as loud as thunder; they had to leave early to catch the last train to Kent and ran down the empty tunnels in the underground singing 'Bennie and the Jets' at the top of their voices. 'Listening to records is one thing,' he tells me. 'But hearing it with thousands of other people is something else.'

Mum and Dad make it absolutely clear I will not be going to London to see Elton John or anyone else for a very long time to come, but in nearby Folkestone is the Leas Cliff Hall and bands come and play there, bands that we read about in *Melody Maker*. Mum and Dad are not at all keen on me going there either and tell me, 'You're only fourteen,' as if that is a reason in itself. Andy and Fred go without me to see a band called the Pink Fairies and come back unharmed with a story of the sound being so loud you could actually feel it through your whole body. They also said the crowd *freaked out*. I think about how embarrassed it makes me to dance at a disco, then remember Mum and Dad having friends for dinner, taking off their shoes and swaying around the living room like beanpoles to the sound of the James Last Orchestra. This new thing, this *freaking out* seems entirely different. In my head, when I'm listening to music, I let go of everything, which is private *freaking out*, and from what Andy and Fred are telling me, this is what actually happens when the crowd *freaks out* together. I have seen snatches of this happening on television, when they show footage of a pop festival, but I have not actually experienced people letting go with complete abandon and not caring what anyone thinks. Even at the disco everyone dances as if someone else is watching. Mum and Dad are not keen but I wear them down and they compromise with an early curfew: they will be outside at ten o'clock on the dot. So, wearing my new cheesecloth shirt and accompanied by Andy and Fred – who have a separate arrangement and will stay until the end – I descend into the hall on Saturday night.

The Leas Cliff Hall is built into the cliffside and has a flat roof on which it is possible to look through a telescope to buildings on the French coast. Inside the whole place is a fug of cigarette smoke and the floors are sticky with beer. The stage dominates the hall and on either side are huge columns of speakers. Although it is dark I can see the stage is crowded with amplifiers and drums. Every now and then a man with long grey hair and a T-shirt walks across and adjusts the controls of one of the amplifiers. 'Roadie,' says Fred.

We are here to see a band called The Enid and I am excited as I've read about them in *Melody Maker*. Fred has already seen The Enid and explains they are a symphonic rock band and I listen to him carefully as he describes how the synthesisers, twin lead guitars and orchestral drum kit all knit together. What I really want to know is when the freaking out will start. 'It might not,' says Fred. 'It's not that sort of music.' We are the youngest people in the hall and I feel very grown up standing with older teenagers who are holding pints and smoking cigarettes. In the bar I join the queue for drinks and cannot believe my luck when I am served a half-pint of pale ale. I drink it so quickly it makes me giddy. Most people are not interested in the support band, who are not very loud, so conversations carry on around us with everyone shouting at each other. When they are finished there is a small round of applause and the band wave at some people they know near the stage. Then there is a pause and we wait while more roadies come on and fiddle with the equipment on stage. A knot of people near the front becomes a crowd and we join them.

It is gone nine when the lights dim, the band walk on and a great cheer goes up around the hall. I am astounded. The Enid look like the most glamorous people I have ever seen. Their leader, Robert John Godfrey, sits at a bank of keyboards in a tailcoat, sounding incredibly posh when he speaks. One of their guitarists, Francis Lickerish, has a mane of golden hair and wears a shirt that looks like it comes from a fairytale. When the band begin to play the sheer noise of it is everything I hoped it would be. The hugeness of the sound makes me feel like I did when I first stepped into Canterbury Cathedral after being used to the village church; bigger than I could ever imagine. We are standing near a column of speakers to the left of the stage and the bass makes my whole body shake as Francis Lickerish hurls himself across the stage with his long hair flying behind him. Time passes and one long number moves into another. The rhythms are constantly changing and although the audience are getting into it, they are listening rather than *freaking out*. Fred tells me to wait for the very end when they will play something special and I will not be disappointed. It is half past nine, quarter to ten, then ten o'clock and the band are nowhere near finishing. Reluctantly, I work my way back through the crowd and out into the night, where Mum and Dad are waiting in the car. My ears are still ringing with symphonic rock as Mum and Dad talk about the sausages they had for supper in front of the television. I imagine being Francis Lickerish, with a mane of golden hair flying behind me as I throw myself about a stage. The next day Andy tells me that for an encore the band played 'Wild Thing', everybody *freaked out* and it was brilliant.

Heartsong, 2015

Just before Christmas I meet *the one*. I have been working at home on a laptop in the living room, singing songs when I take a break, then distracting myself with online adverts for second-hand guitars. One night I see a picture of a strangely shaped acoustic guitar, with a large body and narrow waist. The guitar is a copy of an instrument played by Gordon Giltrap, a virtuoso musician propelled into the mainstream in 1977 with a piece called 'Heartsong', and whose name is often listed among British guitar greats. I look up 'Heartsong' on YouTube and am flipped back to the seventies: Mum and Dad close together on the stripy sofa in the living room, nodding their heads at the start of *Holiday* on BBC1, where 'Heartsong' was the theme tune.

It is half past three the following afternoon and already nearly dark, with Christmas lights flickering in the windows of a street I have passed for years but never entered. Down the road I go and knock on the front door of a modern house. A man called Bob leads me to a living room full of expensive guitars. He picks one and plays a few notes; he is good. He likes collecting guitars but does not perform, he tells me, when I describe the journey I want to undertake. Then, Bob brings out the Vintage Gordon Giltrap, tucked up inside a heavy case. I lift out the guitar and my fingers trace the grain in the pale wood on the body. It feels light in my hands and comfortable on my lap. When I strum the first chord I know I have found *the one*. The sound is effortlessly loud and full of detail. The guitar sings out, has a voice of its own and fills the room. Best of all it costs only £250. I had imagined *the one* would be forever out of reach.

With the new guitar I resolve to finish the songs that have been hanging around in fragments for years. The first was written for my daughter, Poppy. I had been watching a documentary about the singer-songwriter Graham Parker. His band, the Rumour, were great favourites in my late teens. Now he lives in the USA and the programme followed him at home and out on the road. One sequence showed him carrying his own amplifier into a small bar, somewhere in the middle of America. Part way through, he performed a song written for his daughter when she left home. It was called 'Strong Winds', and perfectly captured that point of departure. Straight away I decided to write a song of my own for Poppy, who was headed for university. I took the title of the Graham Parker song as the opening line of my own, wrote the first verse and ground to a halt. Now I work on the song and carry on until it is finished.

'Poppysong'

Strong winds are blowing off the sea
Leaves are falling like early warnings
Of a change that's got to be
Softer light falling on the day
These devotions are fractured emotions
I watch you walk away
And, hey, what seemed like forever
Was just a breath on the winds of May
And taking it together
How quickly the evening passes away
(Chorus)
There's a light in my window
Wherever you may roam this will always be your home
On the beach through the breaking wave
Time is passing but everlasting
These moments that you made
Don't spend your time waiting
For something to arrive
If I could tell you just one thing
It's to know that you're alive
(Chorus)

Johnny B. Goode, 1976

Back in the living room at Whitegates one afternoon, Andy
and I run through the few numbers we have learned so far.
Although I really like listening to their records, I have no
idea what the musicians in The Enid or Genesis actually
play, with changes of key, tempo and wandering guitar riffs,
but I have got the hang of the Chuck Berry song 'Johnny B.
Goode'. I understand twelve-bar blues and like the way you
can speed it up so it becomes rock and roll and play it slightly
differently over and over again in each song. This, I realise, is
how Status Quo make their music. Then, on my little radio
late one night, I hear Dr. Feelgood, a rock and roll band who
seem to be all sharp edges and frantic playing, as though they
are in a hurry to finish every song. What I really like is the
growl that their singer makes with his voice, so I try to do
the same thing. Fred has been observing our progress and
has sat in silence so far, but when we start playing 'Johnny
B. Goode' he taps his foot and nods his head. When I do the
growly voice he smiles and gives me a thumbs-up sign. Then,
for a few seconds, the guitar, voice and plastic buckets lock

together and become a single sound and I smile at Andy, who smiles back. For a moment we are a band and something that seemed out of reach is a little nearer now.

Afterwards, exhausted by our performance, I am lying on the floor and Andy is stretched over the sofa; buckets, drumsticks and guitar are scattered around us. Andy's mum – in the middle of a shift – comes rushing into the room and points at her son's legs sticking out of his shorts on the sofa. 'Look at those two, they're like a pair of sharks,' she says. 'It's a lovely day. Why don't you go outside?' We tell her we are rehearsing. 'Rehearsing for what?'

We both shrug our shoulders. Although I am desperate to strut about on stage, I can't imagine how our buckets and acoustic guitar can be turned into something outside the living room.

'I've got an idea,' says Andy's mum. 'You two can play at the Christmas party for the old people. That gives you six months to get your act together.' I am shocked, but six months is so far away it might as well be ten years.

'Really?' says Andy, sitting up on the sofa and looking a bit worried.

'Yes, really. Making a racket in the lounge isn't going to get you on *Top of the Pops*, is it?' With that, Andy's mum reaches for some keys on the mantelpiece and leaves the room.

'We've got a gig,' I say out loud and Andy nods. I think of the lights going down in the Leas Cliff Hall and Francis Lickerish in his fairytale shirt.

Waves of Fear, 2016

Apart from knowing it is going to happen soon, I still do not have a plan of how to turn the dream into reality. I have learned the songs and now have the guitar, so what is stopping me? Sitting in the kitchen at the beginning of January I face my biggest fear: stage fright. When I was at school I performed in plays and sang in my band without being overwhelmed by anxiety. I would be nervous, but when it came to the moment of performance, nervousness would become excitement. When I went away to take a degree in drama I loved the exhilaration of being in front of an audience. Then, in the second year, I was cast as Henry IV in *Henry IV, Part 1*. The character has to deliver long speeches and I didn't learn them well enough, so when it came to the first performance I forgot my lines. I remember the silence growing after I ran out of words, searching for what came next, finding nothing and thoughts spinning and tumbling until a voice from the wings prompted the next line. There was the shame of facing my fellow actors after the show and the director taking me aside and cutting all he could from my speeches. Although I made it to the end of the run, I started to lose faith in my ability to remember. I tried to avoid performances where I did not have a script in front of me, and as things got worse, stopped acting on stage altogether. I had developed stage fright.

When I started working for BBC Radio 4, I occasionally produced shows recorded in front of an audience and it was part of the job to warm them up, so when the recording began, everyone was primed to whoop, clap and laugh. I didn't get anxious, if what I needed to say was written down in front of me. These performances were, at best, a stolid address. Then, in 1996, I produced a show at the Edinburgh Festival Fringe with the comedian Julian Clary. In my head, as I walked across the city to the Pleasance Theatre, I turned the stolid address into a stand-up routine. There was no time to get nervous and I performed it to several hundred people with no ill effects. The audience were young and willing to laugh, which they did at almost everything I said. Afterwards the head of the Light Entertainment department at the BBC, who was in the audience, told me, 'You should work on the punchlines, but that was quite good.' Unfortunately, those words went to my head and over the next month I did indeed work on the punchlines. Rather too much. What began as a five-minute improvisation grew into a dense twenty-minute monologue.

When a fellow producer told me she was recording a programme before an audience at the Cheltenham Literature

Festival with an esteemed comic novelist, I jumped in and offered to take her place at the warm-up. Looking from the stage of a hotel ballroom towards a sea of white hair, I should have abandoned the routine and returned to my stolid address. But I didn't. Beginning with a double entendre involving Eddie Grundy from *The Archers* and a courgette, I reached a punchline, stopped and waited for the laughter I had been hearing in my head. Julian Clary told me how audience laughter is contagious and builds until continuous waves of sound roll around a theatre. In Cheltenham there was no sound whatsoever and when I scanned the faces in front of me no one was smiling either. The next section of my routine was also met with total silence. Eventually the esteemed comic novelist turned to the actor sitting next to him and said, 'This is shit, how long is it going on for?' As he was sitting in the front row and speaking loudly I could hear every word. 'I don't know,' said the actor, equally loudly, 'but it is fucking awful.' While I continued my routine they carried on having a loud, sweary conversation about how terrible I was. They might as well have shredded my script and thrown the pieces in the air because that was what happened in my head. Eventually I stuttered to a halt and endured a long pause before a man in the crowd shouted, 'I think we're warmed up enough now,' and began a slow handclap. I slunk off stage and into the bar, my face burning with shame. Afterwards, a friend gave me a photograph so I could never forget the evening. I was wearing a white collarless shirt and holding a microphone in one hand. The other arm was up in the air as if I was trying to show how high something was. I remembered, as my jokes fell on increasingly deaf ears, spinning my right arm around in a windmill motion, as if this might unleash the torrent of laughter I had imagined. I stuck the picture on the wall and when anyone asked for an explanation said it was my Icarus moment.

For a while after the Cheltenham incident, I avoided speaking in front of audiences unless what I needed to say was written down. Then when I left my job at the BBC and started writing for a living I was invited to give talks and lectures. To start with I scripted every single word, until I realised I knew what I was talking about and I could just open my mouth and speak. Gradually, the nerves reduced and I enjoyed public speaking. But the fear of public singing has never gone away. Despite the practice and the stealth gigs, the thought of walking on stage to sing a song remains as terrifying as it ever did. And I know, I know, I must do it soon.

Visions of Angels, 1976

I leave the avenue and walk up the path to the village. There is mud underfoot from rain the night before and the ground between the back garden fences is choked with weeds. It is a hot Saturday afternoon in June. In the wallet in the back of my flared jeans is a five-pound note, enough to buy an LP. My musical tastes have become so much more sophisticated now I am a musician myself. I am obsessed with the band Genesis. Their music and lyrics sound like a secret passage to a magical kingdom.

Although it is easier to catch a bus to Folkestone where there is a record shop, I prefer to travel by train, because the train is an adventure. I walk up Sandling Road past the entrance to my school, silent on a Saturday. The occasional car passes, but the road is mostly empty, as are the fields and the distant woods. Almost nothing seems to be moving on this hot day apart from me. At the station the metal on the footbridge is warm to the touch.

I get on the train and that is empty too and nearly all the windows are open, so the clackety racket of the undercarriage is exaggerated, and wafts of scented air transform the smell of the train into summer fields. I walk from Folkestone Central into town, sleepy on this sticky afternoon.

In the dimly lit record shop I am the only customer. I search through the racks, fingers walking the sleeves as I flick through LPs. Occasionally I lift one out to examine the picture, peering through the scratched plastic cover that protects each album. I already have a shortlist of two records I want to buy, so this searching is just exquisite pleasure, prolonging the moment of decision. The racks are arranged in alphabetical order so I give the G section a wide berth, saving it for the end. Within the Gs, the band Genesis have their own sub-section. I want to buy either *Selling England by the Pound* or *Trespass*. The former I have heard at a friend's house while the latter I only know by name. I study the artwork on the cover and read as much of the sleeve notes as is possible through the scratched plastic. I weigh up the known versus the unknown. Then I put both records back and leave the shop.

I walk to the Leas, the ribbon of ornamental gardens that run along the clifftop, and stand staring across the shimmering water to silhouette cliffs on the French coast. The air is full of squawking gulls and the breeze carries the smell of holidays and the faint sound of children playing in the waves far below. My mind is a frenzy of indecision. *Trespass* or *Selling England*… known versus unknown… five pounds… I think of how it will play out on Monday when I'm back at school and tell the story of the weekend.

I go back to the shop and go through the whole thing again. At last I decide. I will take the risk and go for the unknown. It is the blue of the painting on the cover of *Trespass* that decides it, as it seems to match the colour of the sea and the sky. I pass over my five pounds and walk back to the station. Sitting on the empty platform waiting for the train, I pull out the sheet of lyrics from the inner sleeve. The words are shrouded in mystery but hint at something bigger than this hot afternoon in Folkestone, something more mysterious than the small town of Hythe and Mum and Dad mowing the lawn at home.

I Won't Back Down, 2016

It is early January when I open an email from Bristol Old Vic to discover the theatre is celebrating its 250th birthday with some special shows. Among them is a celebration of Bristol's creative spirit, for which they are inviting ideas for a short performance. Straight away I know this is the opportunity I have been waiting for. I have watched the stage of the Bristol Old Vic from the comfort of the audience for so long and the thought of walking onto it alone is both exciting and terrifying. I write a proposal but keep it on my computer. As long as I don't send it off I feel safe. I think of all the years since I last sang a song on stage. I think of time running out and how I will feel if I never sing again. As the deadline approaches I make excuse after excuse to myself. I imagine the humiliation of grinding to a halt mid-song and the sound of my footsteps as I creep off stage in silence. I sit in front of my laptop, finger poised over the send button, then go to the kitchen and make more tea. Finally, as the deadline approaches I close my eyes and press send.

While waiting for a response I can't seem to concentrate, so start messing around with a song I started eight years ago. All I have is a title, a verse and a chorus. It is called 'Brislington Diamonds', Brislington being a suburb of Bristol and the diamonds being glass from a broken windscreen. It is a phrase a Bristolian friend told me ages ago that I brought home and turned into the start of a song, but like so many it stayed as a beginning. Now, it explodes like a word bomb and I cannot say what it is or is not about, it just seems to exist.

'Brislington Diamonds'

The pavement's encrusted with Brislington
    Diamonds
There's a hole in my dash where my sounds
    used to be
There's a hole in my soul that haunts my direction
It's the ghost of yesterday that's coming back for me
Friday night's erupting like a small volcano
On the revved-up streets when the fog comes down
And I get a little shiver when I'm walking by the river
Through the stagged-up dudes of this bare-leg town
I thought by now I would know better than to see the
    world through the bottom of a glass
But with times as good as these why would I care
    whatever comes to pass?

(Chorus)
It's just too good to be true
When will I see the dark side of you?
It's just too good to be true
There's got to be another side, another side of you
The whole street is raging like an overflowing river
And the sleepers in the doorways are a sad
    sight to see
Everything gets loud when I'm running with
    the crowd
Tonight there is no better place that I could be
Then it's close to midnight and I feel a kiss brush
    across my cheek
There's so much I want to say but by now I'm way
    too drunk to speak
(Chorus)
Feeding time for the frenzy tonight
Whisky head and cold cold starlight
Running down these avenues, running through the old
    familiar dreams
(Chorus)

Then, I hear a ping from my computer and the producer from the Old Vic writes back to say I have a ten-minute slot on the main stage in two weeks' time. 'You can always back out,' says one voice in my head. 'No you can't,' says another.

All I have to do is walk on stage, sing a couple of songs and walk off again. Those ten minutes become the border between the present and the future. Anything that happens before the performance I can enjoy thinking about, but anything beyond the border is a murky, twilight world.

Looking for Someone, 1976

Back in my bedroom I remove *Trespass* from the sleeve, hold it at the very edges and lay it, tenderly, on the turntable of my Dansette record player. I lift the arm and lay the needle in the groove. There is the anticipatory crackle that quiets as Peter Gabriel's voice trickles from the single speaker, loaded with secrets and delicious wisdom.

Now I am standing in front of the mirror, curtains pulled so the neighbours cannot see, and mouthing along to the words. It is not myself I see. I am looking through Peter Gabriel's eyes into an ocean of upturned faces, mouths open in adoration, like a nest full of hungry baby birds.

Play That Funky Music, 2016

With the gig coming up at Bristol Old Vic I test my resolve by recording a few songs in a local studio. On the morning of the session I change the strings, pack my leads and straps in the guitar case and walk out into a bright January afternoon with *the one* dangling from my arm.

Although fear stopped me singing live I never stopped recording music. At university, a choreographer asked me to create the soundtrack for a contemporary dance piece to be performed in Winchester Cathedral. I used all my savings to buy a four-track cassette machine called a Portastudio and recorded the whole thing in an abandoned laundry room in my student house. It was incredible to layer one sound on top of another and build up pieces of music, section by section, playing a part over and over again until I got it right. The PR company promoting the event persuaded Casio to give me a synthesiser and an article with my picture appeared in *What Keyboard* magazine. I seemed to be touching the outer reaches of success. A couple of the pieces in the commission were conventional songs for which I developed a vocal style somewhere between talking and singing. I released the project on cassette, selling nearly two hundred copies, many by mail order to people I didn't know. One hot evening towards the end of summer term I was walking through the streets of Winchester and was stopped in my tracks by the sound of my own voice coming from the upper window of a Georgian house. It was the most extraordinary thing to hear my own song spilling into the road and have no idea who lived within the walls. The music had made a small journey across the city and it felt like the beginning of something. It never happened again.

As I climb on the train with my guitar and take a seat on the side of the carriage that overlooks the river, I wonder what will happen to the recordings I am about to make. Who will listen to them and where will they be heard? I allow the fantasy of the songs spreading across the globe on the internet, carried by Twitter and Facebook to homes and hearts around the world.

I get off the train at Montpelier station and walk down through Stokes Croft, past graffiti, abandoned buildings and dapper coffee shops. Glancing in a window to look at a reflection of myself with the guitar case, I see behind the glass to posters and flyers for singers, bands, DJs and songwriters. It is the same in all the windows along the strip; hundreds of names on this stretch of road alone. Then I remember a bleak sight on a wet day in the Gloucestershire town of Cirencester a few months before. I was on my way to run a writing workshop and looked down an alleyway covered from floor to ceiling in posters that flapped in the wind; all local bands vying for attention. I think of every town and city across the country and how many musicians are clamouring to be heard. And here am I, guitar in hand, on my way to a studio to add my voice to the throng.

The city that has been my home for twenty-five years is changing fast. When I came here there were sound systems on the streets of St Pauls, the district that had been the scene of an uprising in 1980. Now, blocks of balconied flats with big glass windows are under construction and the mini marts and fried-chicken shops are in retreat. I am to be one of the last clients of Attic Attack, a little recording studio in a rundown Georgian building in Portland Square. For years this dilapidated property was the home to small creative endeavours, but now it is about to be redeveloped and everyone is on notice to leave. As I stand on the step working out which entryphone button to push, my friend Sarah Moody cycles around the corner, a cello in a soft case strapped to her back. I have asked Sarah to join me in the studio so her mellifluous playing can invigorate the recordings. We walk up the dusty concrete stairs and through rooms lined with ancient cinematic equipment until we are met by Pete Rowley, the genial sound engineer and studio owner.

Attic Attack is in the middle of the building, so there is no natural light. The control room is a little booth with racks full of old analogue equipment, most of which doesn't get used now everything is recorded on a computer. There is a battered sofa at the back of the room, opposite a lava lamp and digital sound desk in front of the window that looks into the studio itself. Pete leads us to where a double bass, missing two of its strings, leans against the blue-carpeted wall. We sit on office chairs and I play Sarah the songs as microphones are set up around us. We start with 'Poppysong' and straight away Sarah finds a cello part that supports the tune in places, echoes it in others and emphasises the guitar riff between verses. As this is the start of my new musical life, I decide to record each song in one live take – there will be no overdubs. I have to play the guitar, sing and co-ordinate with Sarah all at once. While we are practising it all seems very natural, but when Pete's voice comes over the intercom to tell us he is recording, everything changes. I am aware of my hands and voice before the unforgiving microphone. The more I think about it, the more mistakes I make. Pete must see this sort of thing all the time, and is never anything less than encouraging, excited to have a cello in the mix. I gradually stop thinking and just do it. I have been playing these songs over and over for the last year, so once I relax, my fingers and voice know what to do by themselves. We record four songs that afternoon and when I get home and play them back I know, for the first time in my life, I can do this. I just have to walk on that stage and sing.

She Bangs the Drums, 1976

Now it is the week before Christmas. We carry our equipment into the canteen that is decorated with bunting and strings of cards. There is always an odour of disinfectant at Whitegates but today it has been overwhelmed by the smell of Christmas dinner. Fred has already lent us his amplifier and as we set up he walks into the room with his Fender Stratocaster as well, the beautiful instrument given by his parents that I have worshipped from afar. 'You've got to have a decent guitar for your first gig,' he says, handing me the case. Andy's drum kit has grown too; he has managed to supplement the bucket with a military drum and a cymbal. I have taped a microphone from a cassette recorder onto a broom handle so it looks like we have a microphone stand.

As we set up the residents shuffle in for the Christmas party. They pull crackers and put on paper hats. Some are curious and come up close to investigate while others watch us warily from tables on the other side of the room. The meal is served while jolly Christmas music plays in the background. I sit on the amplifier and look out at our audience as they tuck into turkey and sprouts. It is not what I imagined when I imagined our first gig. Also, I am nervous and it is a new feeling; when I watch *Top of the Pops* it never occurs to me the groups might be frightened, as everyone is always smiling and looking so happy as they jump about. But there it is in the base of my tummy, that feeling: nerves. As I wait to begin I cross and uncross my legs, not knowing what to do with myself, wanting to appear cool but just being nervous.

'We've got a special treat for you tonight,' says Andy's mum. 'Or at least I hope we have. It's the first time they've ever played in front of an audience. Please give a big warm welcome to my son and his friend... They are called... the Entangled Network.' I know we should launch straight into a song but my guitar is out of tune. I was so nervous I forgot to tune up. So I stand there doing it now while Andy bashes the cymbal and hits the military drum. We sound like a strange experimental jazz combo and the old people look at each other and wonder if we have begun yet. Then we do, with our version of the Chuck Berry song 'Johnny B. Goode'.

There is a difference between imagining a performance and actually doing it. That is what I realise in this moment. In my mind I am slick, not having to try too hard as music flows from my fingertips. It is as though all my shortcomings will magically resolve once there are people in front of me. I'd thought performing music would be a more intense version of listening to it; now I'm not so sure.

Despite only having one amplifier into which both the guitar and microphone are plugged, we are very loud and I see a lady on the nearest table screwing up her face and putting her fingers in her ears. Then others do the same. Many of them were born when Queen Victoria was on the throne and have lived through two world wars. Now tonight, at a Christmas party, they are being assaulted by this terrible noise. I start to run up and down a bit, remembering Francis Lickerish on stage at the Leas Cliff Hall, but I can only go a couple of feet when I run out of guitar lead and have to stop. I make faces at Andy and then to the audience, the grimace that I have seen on TV when pop stars are really into their music. One man shakes his head, pulls himself up on his walking frame and heads for the door. Others follow and I watch their slow-motion exit. One lady stands up and tries to dance and clap along, but finds it hard to locate the rhythm in the mush of sound. Then, as the last beat of the military drum ends 'Wild Thing', our final number, there is applause from the few remaining elderly people who were too polite to leave.

That's Entertainment, 2016

I wake in the dark. It is 6:30 a.m. My first thought is how easy it would be to send an email to the theatre saying I am ill and put an end to this. I make a cup of tea and bring it back to bed and with rain hammering against the window, rehearse the songs in my head. Pulling on a pair of shorts and T-shirt, I go out running through the wet morning; up the stony path between the gardens of the big houses in Sneyd Park and on to the open space of Bristol Downs. As I run, anxiety melts away leaving gentle euphoria in its wake. Back home I pick up my guitar and practise the first song. I visualise success: looking to the balconies of the theatre and smiling faces looking back; bowing at the end; applause ringing around the auditorium as I walk to the safety of the wings. Then Sarah arrives at the house and we go to the Co-op for tomatoes and an avocado, which are the only things I can imagine eating.

At two o'clock precisely I hold up my guitar case and thread my way through the crowded foyer of the Bristol Old Vic. People are already queuing from the auditorium doors back to the entrance and I start to feel nervous again; I had secretly hoped no one would come and I would sing to an empty theatre. I check in and am taken to the upstairs bar that is the artists' waiting area, but I am the only artist there, so pace up and down until a storyteller arrives and we exchange a nervous hello. From downstairs the level of murmuring increases as more people arrive. Because this is a big show with lots of performers taking part, I have been allocated an artist liaison person, Jo, to make sure I am in the right place at the right time. Now she rushes in, briefs me on what will happen before running backstage with my guitar, leaving me in the bar with my coat and damp hands.

Five minutes of floor pacing later and I am called to the stage for a soundcheck. It looks like chaos with technicians, a folk band and a choir all setting up at once. I wander to and fro across the stage and peer out to the galleried seating, as though I know what I am doing and am sizing up the space for the performance ahead.

'Can we do a line check on the guitar?' A disembodied voice comes from an invisible speaker and a technician takes the end of my guitar lead and plugs me in. I strum the opening chords of the first song. This is only the second time I have plugged in this guitar and it sounds completely different coming out of the speakers of a great big theatre.

'Don't need a mic check, do we?' The disembodied voice speaks again and everyone on stage looks in my direction.

'No, that's fine,' I say.

'Great, all done then.' My guitar is unplugged and the cable curled up and taken to the wings.

'You can watch the show from the upper circle if you like,' says Jo. 'I'll come and get you before you're on.'

So here I am, sitting in the dark with five hundred other people. Way below me on the stage of the Bristol Old Vic are the Gurt Lush Choir, filling the theatre with the most beautiful sound. I start to count them but when I reach forty-eight there is a tap on my shoulder. 'It's time. Follow me. I'll take you round the back.' I stand up and do what I'm told. We pass through narrow corridors and down winding staircases to emerge in the wings. It is dark there now and I breathe in the backstage smell of woodyard mingled with the distant bouquet of fresh paint. The backstage crew are all wearing black and talking quietly into headsets. I can see out onto the stage, and when the choir finishes there is a wave of applause so loud it makes me step back into the darkness.

Jo creeps up and whispers in my ear. 'OK, Paul, stand by.'

I strap on my guitar and wipe sweaty palms on my trousers. In the middle of the stage is the compère. 'Ladies and gentlemen, our next act is here to sing. He's wanted to do this for a long time and from today he's out on the road not taken. Please give a big round of applause for Paul Dodgson.' People start clapping and the compère walks off.

I remain rooted to the spot and Jo whispers again. 'Paul. That's your cue. Have a great one. Smash it!'

I take the long slow walk out to centre stage thinking 'smash it?' Oh yes, that's what young people say, meaning hope it goes well. The lights are so bright the auditorium is invisible. I can see the front row and straight away spot a man I have never spoken to but have seen around Bristol for years. In fact I have seen him for so long I have watched his hair turn grey. I am standing there thinking, 'It's you, with the grey hair, what are you doing here?' And he is looking at me and thinking, 'It's you, with the grey hair, what are you doing here?' Then I realise he is waiting for something to happen, as are all the other people in the theatre.

I give the guitar an exploratory strum and hear the chord ring out from the auditorium speakers. I start to talk, saying whenever I play an amplified guitar I expect to hear my mum telling me to get on with my homework. From the darkness beyond the stage lights comes a modest ripple of laughter. Then I play a little instrumental piece designed to settle my nerves and have an out-of-body experience. Nothing like this has ever happened to me in my whole life before, but for a moment I am looking down from above, watching hands on the fretboard and thinking, 'It's me doing this, making this sound.' It is so strange to be on this stage with all these people watching me, and so unlike the version I imagine, when I am as relaxed as the middle of a perfect holiday. Instead, I am hyperaware of every tiny sound in the audience, the heat of the stage lights and the minute changes in the facial expressions of the people in the front row.

I introduce the first song by explaining why I didn't do this thirty years ago, following a script I have written and memorised.

'I was too scared, too scared to commit,' I say. 'To this road with no route map, to the possibility of not being good enough, to the chance it would all go wrong. I got a proper job instead.' Then, on the spur of the moment, I ad lib. 'If you can call working for the BBC a proper job.' There is another modest ripple of laughter and as I wait for it to subside, I cannot remember what I am supposed to say next. The silence that follows opens up and is almost vertiginous. Then I remember. 'I'm going to sing a song now,' I say. 'It was written by Emmylou Harris and is called "Boulder to Birmingham".'

The introduction is two bars long and the vocal begins without guitar on the third beat of the third bar. When I start to sing I hear my voice amplified by the speakers in the theatre, sounding huge, bigger than me, as big as all the time I have waited for this to happen. I know what is coming from my mouth is not perfect, that this won't be one of those *X Factor* moments when the audience leap to their feet with tears in their eyes. But that doesn't matter because I am actually singing. With my eyes wide open staring into the dark, I wish I had practised with the microphone as this inflated sound is so unfamiliar. I move on and off the microphone looking for the right place but the words are all there and I stick to the tune. After the first chorus it feels like a downhill run to the end of the song and as the last chord dies there is a wave of warm applause from the darkness.

On firmer ground now and halfway through, I put the guitar on its stand, pick up the shruti box and introduce 'Coal Not Dole'. I start up the drone, close my eyes, start to sing again and as I do, realise I am actually enjoying this whole thing. Then, like the crew of a ship who smell a new land from far out to sea, I sense what life will be like when this is over. At the end of the song I experience surging relief and intoxicating joy. I hear a small whoop – probably Sarah – amid applause that carries on while I take a bow, straighten up, smile into the darkness and walk off the stage.

After the show at the Old Vic I am on a high that lasts the rest of the day. The streets that were drab and grey on my way to the theatre are vibrant and full of colour as we drive to a falafel restaurant in Clifton, where the food is so full of flavour, it is as though I have discovered taste for the first time.

In his book *Instrumental*, the concert pianist James Rhodes, who came late to performance, describes the experience of his first recital, at the age of thirty-three. 'It goes well. A few fluffed notes, no major memory lapses (I still have a recording of it), decent voicing (where the melody sings out properly), new (to me) musical interpretations of pieces that have been played for centuries. And I realise that all of those fantasies about giving concerts that I had as a kid, that kept me alive and safe in my head, were accurate. It really is that powerful. And I knew I wanted to do it for ever. No matter what.' And that is exactly how I feel today.

I had not advertised my appearance in case it all went wrong, but later in the evening I announce my 'coming out' as a performer on Facebook, and receive congratulatory messages and offers of gigs. Within a couple of days I have shows set up around the country and will be out on the road in the months to come. To begin with I will play low-key events as a support act, but by May I need to be ready to carry a whole gig on my own. As this happens the anxiety returns, or at least the memory of anxiety. I consult the wisdom of my old friend Fred. 'Concentrate on the singing and the playing and not the audience,' he tells me. 'Take something of the rehearsal room into the show.'

It's All Too Much, 1976

On 18 December 1976, a proper rock star comes to town and I get a flavour of what life could be like once we have paid our dues on the old people's Christmas party circuit. It is Saturday night, the Leas Cliff Hall is packed, and Mum and Dad have agreed to let me stay to the end. I have managed to consume two pints of beer and freaked out so much to the support band that a girl from the grammar school – two years older and someone I have watched from afar – tapped me on the shoulder and asked if I was having a fit. Andy, Fred and I are standing near the front, the place I always like to be, and I turn around and look across the crowded floor to the packed balcony. The lights go down and in the semi-darkness musicians come on to the stage. A chant begins behind me and grows around the hall. 'Hillage, Hillage, Hillage, Hillage...' Then the lights come up on Steve Hillage standing in the middle of the stage, looking exactly as I imagine Jesus would if he played a Fender Stratocaster. He has long nut-brown hair, a beard, clothes like robes and a beneficent smile. The band start to play and I lose myself in the music. Whenever Steve Hillage performs a guitar solo (and he does quite a few of these) he never looks at his fingers, just out into the audience with a radiant smile on his face. Last night the band played at the Hammersmith Odeon and *L*, Steve's latest record, has been riding high in the album charts. Hardly anyone at school knows about him, so it feels like we are in on a secret. When the band start to play their version of the George Harrison number 'It's All Too Much', the whole crowd leaps up and down to the infectious riff at the heart of the song and I am swept up in such intense joy that I am left soaking wet, exhausted and deliriously happy when the lights come on at the end of the gig.

On Christmas Day Andy calls to tell me he was given a drum kit as his main present. As soon as I can get away I go to see him. The drums have been set up in his little bedroom and take up most of the space. I sit on the drumstool and look at the view of the tom-tom, snare, bass drum and cymbals, imagining looking out to the crowd at the Leas Cliff Hall. Then we swap places and Andy picks up his sticks and plays a simple rhythm. I close my eyes and savour the thought that we are already in a different league to the amateurs who played the Whitegates Christmas party just two weeks ago. We are on our way.

Goodbye England (Covered in Snow), 2016

There are three weeks before the next performance. My friend Jem, whom I have known since Poppy and Fred were born and has children of the same age, presents a world music show on a community radio station in the Somerset town of Glastonbury. He, along with other presenters from the station, are organising a day-long festival. When I tell people I am playing at Glastonbury they assume it is at the big festival up the road. No, I explain, this is called Glastonbury Calling and is highlighting local bands and artists. Jem has invited me to open the festival with a thirty-minute set in the Riflemans Arms, a pub on the edge of town. In the weeks that follow, when talking about the gig, I use the phrase 'open the festival', rather than 'the bottom of a very big bill'. Spin has always been a necessary evil in popular music.

I want to use three different tunings – open D, DADGAD and standard tuning – and buy a pedal tuner that sits on the floor in front of me, with a visual display to indicate when each note is in tune. I can just about retune by ear, but am frightened that some smart arse with perfect pitch will spring out of the audience to tell me my tuning is all wrong. I practise changing tunings almost as much as I practise singing songs, remembering my debut with the Entangled Network and how fiddling about killed the show before we had even begun. I know I could easily have another guitar on stage ready tuned, but I am wedded to the image of the lone troubadour with a single guitar, travelling down the road to his next gig.

Back in my kitchen running through my repertoire, I understand how hard it is to keep practising, to keep playing the same thing day after day. I think about all the musicians I see on stage, how effortless they make it look, and wonder if they are secreted in their kitchens right now, running through songs over and over again. Two years ago the improvement seemed so rapid I could surprise myself from one day to the next, but now I cannot tell if I am getting better or worse. Sometimes I imagine the esteemed comic novelist from the Cheltenham Literature Festival in front of me saying, 'This is shit. How long is it going on for?' But I carry on, singing the same songs over and over again, my only defence against what is to come.

The following weekend the BBC Radio 6 Music Festival is held at various venues in the centre of Bristol. On Sunday afternoon I am sitting down in my kitchen and gazing at the early evening sky as Frank Turner comes on stage in a nightclub down the road. As 'Get Better' surges out of the radio and fills up the kitchen, I am forced onto my feet. I have been feeling hopeless all day, but thirty seconds into the first song I remember why I want this too.

Sarah and I have tickets to the festival's closing session and head off to the Colston Hall. The headline act is Laura Marling who is only twenty-six years old and already a doyenne of subtle, dark love songs in unusual tunings; she uses different guitars, I note, and a guitar technician does the actual tuning work off stage. Laura Marling comes on wearing a cream-coloured jumper and chalk-white skirt. With her short blonde hair, pale face and habit of tilting her head back as she plays, Laura Marling is an ethereal presence among the swooping television cameras, strings of lanterns and trees that dress the stage. Her voice is a soaring instrument that packs an emotional punch and I close my eyes to let the music wash through me and as I do so, all anxiety melts away. It is dreamlike. Marling's lyrics and melodies offer glimpses of a hinterland, bigger than the song itself and just out of reach, as though a door opens to a view of a distant landscape.

When she sings one of her best known songs, 'Goodbye England (Covered in Snow)', I am taken back six years to hearing it on a day in January, when it seemed all England was one giant snowfield and I listened to the song over and over again on a slow train journey. The nuances of Laura Marling's music seemed to fit perfectly with my melancholy mood and the song became the perfect soundtrack to the day as I listened through headphones while we crawled from Bristol to Cheltenham via Swindon, until the melancholy underwent a transfiguration into joy.

Laura Marling's songs are like partially told stories. There are gaps to fill and that is why the song seemed to be written for me on that snowy day. When I first started listening to rock music I used to search the songs for meaning, but now I project meaning onto them. I am selective in the lyrics I receive and weave my own narrative. Hearing 'Goodbye England (Covered in Snow)' brings it all back, the melancholy and the joy and everything that has happened since in one big wave of emotion. And all these feelings are so much more intense because the song is being sung live a few feet away from me. I sit in my seat with tears running down my face hoping nobody can see me crying. It is strange that as a boy brought up not to cry, it is only music that unlocks the shutters and lays bare the emotions within. This, this is what a song can do. As the writer, singer, songwriter and half of Everything But The Girl, Tracey Thorn says in her book about singing, *Naked at the Albert Hall*: 'Songs, then, allow us to sing things we can't say.'

Laura Marling's show is like a warm embrace that lingers long after the gig has ended. I know I will never be able to do what I have just seen and heard. I will never have her dexterity with the guitar, never have a voice that soars through the upper register and will never write enough songs to be able to play for an hour and fifteen minutes of the very best from my many albums. I would, though, like to write at least one song that makes someone cry.

In the days that follow I think about something that happened at the gig. About a third of the way through her set, she forgot the words to a song and stopped. She paused for a moment, said, 'Sorry, it's been a while,' and carried on. It happened so quickly that half the audience probably didn't even notice. What interested me was the way she kept her composure. One of my great fears is forgetting lyrics – probably a throwback to my days as Henry IV – and yet here was Laura Marling singing in front of fifteen hundred people in the hall and live on national radio and television, forgetting her words and carrying on as if it was no big deal. There was no sign of panic. When I'm practising and forget the words, my brain goes into a frenzy as I chase the elusive lyric to corners of my mind where it slips through a trapdoor and disappears into the night.

Let There Be Rock, 1977

When Nana and Grandad come to stay I make them sit through a concert by the heavy rock band AC/DC. There is so little rock music on BBC or ITV that I commandeer the television whenever something is shown, despite Mum and Dad continuing to shake their heads in disbelief. I sit through cheesy variety shows, hoping that a proper rock band will slip through the net and play a screaming guitar solo amid the comedians and dancers, but all I ever see are chart bands and their false smiles. My friends at school talk about a programme called *The Old Grey Whistle Test* that takes rock music seriously and has bands playing in the studio, but it's on late at night, after the curfew when Mum and Dad insist the television is turned off.

Tonight's programme is being broadcast on both radio and television simultaneously, so I switch on the TV, tune in the radiogram and turn up the volume. The first song is called 'Let There Be Rock', which builds slowly, and I keep inching the volume up until Mum, who is in the kitchen next door, comes into the room and tells me to turn it down. Grandad looks on in horror as Angus Young – the lead guitarist, who is dressed as a schoolboy with shorts and a cap – runs around the stage, and the singer – all muscles and a denim waistcoat – sounds as if he is continually screaming. But what really annoys Grandad is the drumming. 'There's no subtlety,' he says. 'Look at him thrashing down every beat of the bar.' I laugh. 'It's rock and roll, Grandad,' I say in a mock hippy drawl that I hope is a passable imitation of Keith Richards of the Rolling Stones. Because I'm so busy laughing, I don't ask Grandad about the drummer in his band, how they got together, what songs they sang, where they played and why they broke up. Grandad's band doesn't seem to have any connection with the Entangled Network. They are irrelevant.

Meanwhile, in distant London, a new musical movement is born. Boys and girls a few years older than us pick up electric guitars and start to play, celebrating their lack of proficiency. We see their snarling, spotty faces in the pages of the music press and occasionally hear their songs on late night Radio 1. The music sounds simple, angry and violent. Although no punk rockers come anywhere near Hythe, something of their spirit infects us. You don't have to be a brilliant musician, they say from afar, you just have to do it.

I'm Not Sleeping, 2016

As the days pass and the date of Glastonbury Calling gets nearer, I start losing sleep. I wake early, worrying about work, the house, everything. That passes at dawn and I know what I am really worrying about is the gig. One day I go for a long run in the morning, cycle into Bristol in the evening, speed home under a cold, starlit sky, fall asleep on the stairs taking off my shoes, drag myself to bed just after midnight and wake bolt upright at four. By five I am downstairs washing up and listening to the shipping forecast. No matter how many times I tell myself it is a gig in a pub and there will hardly be anyone there, the anxiety haunts my nights and days.

Things get better on the Wednesday before Glastonbury Calling, when I appear, by phone, on Jem's radio show. I have spent much of my adult life working on radio programmes and have been all over the world to make them, but there is no more pleasurable moment than hearing Jem introduce 'Poppysong' and the music starting to play. Because the station is transmitted in the Glastonbury area and streamed on the internet, I have to listen on my computer in Bristol, and turn it off before the song ends, so I don't create a feedback loop when I speak. I pace the stripped floorboards of the living room wearing slippers, phone pressed against my ear, as Jem asks what I am doing, why I am doing it and what it means to do something I have always wanted to do. The more I speak, the more it seems to make sense: the practice, the nerves, the need to make my own music, the desire to make a mark. And as I talk I know that in Kent, Mum is listening on her iPad, Sarah at an easel in a life-drawing class in Wales, and my son Fred and his mum gathered around a computer in North Somerset.

Slap That Bass, 1977

Now Andy has a proper drum kit, Fred joins the band. Although practice has improved my playing, there are other mysterious qualities beyond my grasp. I know Fred will bring these to the Entangled Network. It isn't just the way he plays, it is the way he hears music too: he can work out a song by listening to it on a record, whereas for me, music is noise until someone shows me the chords.

We have our first band meeting in Andy's living room and Fred insists on two big changes. Because Fred is a guitarist and much better than me, he wants me to play the bass. This comes as quite a shock as it was only recently I noticed a bass guitar had four strings and have no idea how to play one. Fred explains that a bass is like the bottom four strings of a guitar and he will tell me what notes to play. 'The big advantage,' he says, 'is only having to play one note at a time.' Also Fred has a bass he can lend me. I have not paid much attention to bass players in bands, as they do not seem glamorous compared to guitarists. In fact, the more I think about it, I cannot remember the faces of any of the bass players I have seen, as they are usually in the shadows to the side of the drums. Before I can raise any objections, Fred tells me that Paul McCartney is a bass player, which leads us to the matter of singing. 'Although your growling's fine for rock and roll, it'd be better if we had someone who could actually sing,' says Fred. 'Then we can expand the repertoire.' I say I could learn to sing properly, but Fred thinks I will be busy enough practising the bass. Anyway, he has already asked Matthew, who is an ex-choirboy and is known for having a *good voice*.

Born Making Noise, 2016

When I was on stage at Bristol Old Vic, I was surprised by the sound of my voice through the speakers and the different dynamics of an amplified guitar, so a couple of days before Glastonbury Calling I book two hours in a rehearsal room. Dockside Studios is on the first floor of an old industrial building and I look out of a dirty window to the boatyard, marina and brightly painted houses on the hill across the harbour. Steve – one of the studio owners – fiddles with the PA controls and tries to make the reverb work. He can't and leaves me alone in a little room with blue acoustic tiles on the walls and PA speakers suspended from the ceiling. In the kitchen, the subtle changes of pressure applied to the strings means the volume increases subtly and blends with the ambient acoustic of the room. In the rehearsal space I am surprised by the sudden increase in loudness. It all sounds so harsh and every mistake and wrong note is amplified too. It is ironic that forty years after I craved amplification, I have to learn to be loud again. I run through song after song, discovering how far to be from the microphone and how hard to strike the guitar. In quieter songs I learn to sing in a whisper and still be audible. This is exciting, as the dynamic range – the quietest to the loudest sounds – can be enhanced, which means variety for anyone listening; something I cannot achieve in the kitchen. The loudest songs are the hardest to control and I fight the volume of the guitar by raising the level of my voice. I am not breathing properly and start to cough. The last half hour is spent running through the set list, one song straight into another, and by the end both my fingers and throat are hurting. I have new admiration for Bruce Springsteen, Peter Gabriel and everyone else I've seen on stage belting it out for over two hours without a break.

Cum On Feel the Noize, 1977

Suddenly there are twice as many of us in the band and it takes a lot longer to decide anything. For musical matters we defer to Fred, who knows best, but everything else – the songs we should play, who is going to talk between songs, what we should wear, etc. – have to be discussed and agreed by us all. Sometimes, at school, the four of us huddle together at break times and other boys say, 'The band are planning their world tour.' They sound sarcastic but I suspect they are secretly jealous as none of them can play anything. Matthew fits in well. To begin with everything is new so he does what Fred tells him, then after a while he starts to have ideas of his own. Sometimes I detect a tension between the two of them but ignore it, as I so badly want the band to work.

We store our equipment in a cupboard at one end of Whitegates. Before a rehearsal we load everything onto a trolley and push it through muted corridors to the day room on the other side of the complex, where Andy's mum and dad allow us to rehearse in the evenings and at weekends. We push the trolley as fast as we can, riding it, laughing and joking all the way. Sometimes the old people stand at the entrances to their rooms, supported by their walking frames, and silently watch us pass. I can't help thinking that old age is bad luck that happens to other people. When we have set up we talk about what we are going to do for a long time before we actually do it. The day room overlooks the park and on sunny weekend afternoons I open the windows so everyone can hear our noise.

Tuning up is another mystery. I have learned to use the lowest string on the guitar as a reference point and put a finger behind the fifth fret, making the tone of the next string, so the two can be compared. This works for all apart from the G string, where the finger is placed on the fourth fret for reasons I do not understand. Sometimes the guitar gets so far out of tune I cannot bring it back again and have to resort to my pitch pipes to make the note for each string. Fred can of course tune a guitar without effort. He looks into the middle distance, head to one side, long hair hanging down and instructs me to turn the pegs: 'Up a bit, down a bit, up again, that's it.'

Enjoy Yourself (It's Later Than You Think), 2016

Then it is Friday afternoon and I am keeping out of the rain by sitting at a desk in Bristol Central Library and failing to write a play. In fact I cannot concentrate on anything at all. The stage fright is back. It is no exaggeration to say I feel as a prisoner might, who has been sentenced to death and the execution is tomorrow. It is actually the day before Glastonbury Calling. Instead, I sit thinking about why I am so anxious. It seems ridiculous that after waiting thirty-four years to sing, I should feel quite so grim about singing. But then, perhaps I wasn't waiting but putting it off, knowing how it would feel once I stepped towards the stage. While being a troubadour was a fantasy locked up in the safety of my head, I could be the most amazing live performer there was. Now I am living the dream, I will discover how good – or bad – I really am.

Back home I run through songs. Despite all the practice it is still taking ages to move from one tuning to the next, so

I give up for now, deploy the Martin and have two guitars on stage. The image of lone troubadour on the road with a single guitar will have to come later. And anyway, Sarah is driving us to the gig.

I do not get to sleep until one then wake up again at five and run through lyrics at speed in my head while waiting for dawn. I remember everything, which is a relief as last night I forgot the words to two songs. I go for a run at seven, pushing myself further than usual on this cold and cloudy morning. As I move the anxiety melts away until it is a small and manageable thing tucked in the back of my mind. Sarah arrives and eats a croissant in the kitchen as I write a set list. Most of the songs will be my own, with a couple of folk numbers and 'Boulder to Birmingham' thrown in too. I experience a little surge of pleasure in knowing enough songs to have to choose which ones to play. We leave Bristol and the sun comes out as we cross the Mendip Hills. Now it feels like a big adventure, going off to play songs in another town. Then somewhere near Chewton Mendip I forget the lyrics again.

The Riflemans Arms is a pub on the outskirts of Glastonbury and one of four venues hosting gigs at today's festival. I carry my guitars into a modest back room as Pat, the engineer, sets up sound equipment. There is no stage and there are no lights. We have arrived so early there is nothing for me to do, so we walk into town and have a pot of tea. I cannot taste a thing. Back at the venue I am calm and relaxed as I soundcheck, despite the audience already being there and watching from the sides and back of the room. There is a big empty space in front of me. Then I am introduced by Ian – one of the organisers – who says, 'Paul Dodgson is very talented and quite good-looking too.' This gets a big laugh and I resist the temptation to start making jokes and launch straight into the first number. This is now *the performance*, even though I am playing to the same bunch of people who were watching *the soundcheck* moments ago. Then I was relaxed, now I am thinking about every note I play. I start with a fast number, 'Brislington Diamonds'. People twitch to the rhythm and when I get to the chorus a few heads nod. At the end of the song there are a couple of whoops mixed in with the applause and I do a little jump in the air to coincide with the final chord.

Because it is daylight and I am in the back room of a pub, I can see everything and everyone and have the same hyperawareness I experienced at the Old Vic, but happily, no out-of-body experience. There are perhaps thirty people watching and I am aware of the expression on every face. Some are smiling encouragingly, but some look deadly serious and I see their attention wander as they look through the window to the sky. I see every pair of glasses, every scarf and every pint held in every hand. Pub life continues beyond the bar and there I hear voices funnelled through the narrow corridor that separates the two spaces. From somewhere comes a noise sounding like plates being stacked. There is a point, two-thirds of the way through the set, when I start to enjoy myself. I relish being loud and I like being the centre of attention. Announcing the change of guitars I say, 'This is a Martin, but not a very expensive one.' There are two boys sitting on a bench to my right and I hear one of them say to the other, 'No, it isn't.' The tune that follows is an instrumental and on the spur of the moment I ask people to stamp their feet in time with the rhythm. Everyone does immediately and they keep going throughout the song so this moment of participation makes me think it is all going well. Then the PA stops working and I grind to a halt. Pat the soundman says loudly, 'Great, now the DI boxes are all fucked.' While he scrambles around on the floor I step forward and carry on without amplification. The audience seem to enjoy this and the energy in the room goes up a notch. Then, with the PA fixed I play the last song and it is over. There is applause and cheering and I feel euphoria that lasts the rest of the weekend.

As I pack my guitar back in its case someone comes up to me and says, 'Your lyrics are wicked, mate.' And I glow a little. Then Ian gives me £20, telling me he wants all the acts to be paid, even if it is only a small amount. I put the note in my wallet thinking this is the first money I have ever made from singing my own songs. As I am about to leave the next act arrives. He is young, maybe not even twenty, and takes a Martin guitar out of a hard case. Pat the soundman sees it is one of the more expensive guitars in the range and says, 'Oooh, look at you.' The young guitarist perches on a stool and practises complex, lyrical flourishes, as I walk into the afternoon, having opened the festival, at the bottom of the bill.

(How Much Is) That Doggie in the Window?, 1977

I now have a Saturday job at a jeweller's in Folkestone, and during my lunch hour make regular forays around town, disappearing into second-hand bookshops to find old Penguin paperbacks for 10p. At the back of Bouverie Square is a junk shop. The windows are dirty and inside is a dark cave filled with the clutter of house clearances. There are unloved Bakelite radios, boxes of scratched records and dusty shelves of rubbish. It smells like old carpets. I have bought a couple of books in here before and have never seen anything else I want, but love searching for treasure just in case. One Saturday lunchtime I walk through the door and see, hanging on the wall at the back of the shop, like bright berries on a winter tree, a red Höfner Verithin semi-acoustic bass guitar. I take it down and carry it to the window where there is more light. The guitar is beautiful to hold, painted bright red and made of thin wood, which means it is not heavy when hung around my neck. The pickups are silver and the volume controls jet black. The strings are old but even so it is easy to play. When I ask the price, the owner takes the guitar from me and looks it up and down. He has not shaved for days and I watch grey bristles on his chin twitching as he thinks. I expect the guitar to be way out of my reach, in fact I know I will not be able to afford it so brace myself for disappointment. The man rubs some dust off the headstock and spins it around.

'I don't know, mate,' he says. 'Thirty pounds?'

A tingle passes through my body. For once it is useful not to show what I am thinking. The guitar is so obviously undervalued.

'I'll have it,' I say, as casually as possible, and arrange to come back the following week when I have borrowed the money.

Jesus is a Hedgehog, 2016

I write out a set list and eat a bowl of lentil soup and pasta. There is a gig in a couple of hours and I am not anxious. Well, I am a bit, but it is like being touched by a light wind rather than blown by a heavy gale. Last night I slept well and even managed to work on my play for a couple of hours. Then, running through songs in the kitchen, I discover I am actually enjoying the thought of the gig. This evening I will open the bill at the Thunderbolt, a Victorian pub turned music venue out on the Bath Road in Bristol. Dave, the landlord, is an unsung hero of the music business, giving support slots to young groups, who get a taste of playing with lights and sound. The headline act is my friend Kid Carpet. He had seen my Facebook posts and invited me onto the bill.

Kid Carpet – real name Ed Patrick – is a lo-fi genius who writes intensely catchy tunes made with Casio keyboards, children's toys and offbeat noises. After plugging away on the gigging circuit for years he discovered his alter ego was the perfect narrator of anarchic children's theatre, so now he does both, but tonight he is topping the bill for his almost grown-up audience.

The pavement is wet and traffic heavy on the Bath Road as I walk to the venue. I pass an abandoned car lot and look out across a wasteland to the bright lights of Temple Meads station and the city beyond. Outside the Thunderbolt I see names of up-and-coming bands alongside old punks, still out on the road doing it forty years later. I wonder, if I had been performing all these years, whether the road would have led me here too. I was a late addition to the bill so my name isn't on the poster, but it is online and I have clicked the link over the last few days, just for the pleasure of seeing my name listed as a musician.

Being a support act is one of the ways an emerging artist can get experience of playing live and exposure to new audiences. The hope is that some of those watching will like what they hear enough to come back next time. Increasingly, being a support act is unpaid, which is why you often see bands working the merch stall at gigs, because that is the only money they are going to make. Obviously, I would really like my name to be on the poster in big letters and find it hard to admit I am a beginner, but that is what I am. It has taken the pressure off because, unlike some of the gigs I have coming up, almost no one will be here to see me.

The Thunderbolt has a small stage at one end of an L-shaped room with a bar at the back. There are already people drinking when I am invited to soundcheck. I shake hands with Mark, who is doing the sound tonight, and he plugs me into the powerful PA system. Tonight, for the first time, I have stage monitors – on-stage speakers, angled toward my ears, to give me a different sound mix to the one going to the audience – and we work on my personal sound before Mark turns on the PA speakers and sets the levels for the room. I strum a single chord and it is so loud drinkers at the bar stop talking and look. I play little bits of several songs and Dave the landlord gives me a thumbs-up from halfway back, where he is standing with Gary – who goes by the stage name of DJ Cactus County – who will be introducing the acts and playing records in between.

It is hard to know what to do between soundcheck and showtime. Dave keeps offering me beer – free drinks are my fee – but I am driving and want to save the pleasure of a single pint for afterwards. The dressing room is a small cupboard off the back of the stage and is full of equipment, so all I can do is stand in there and read the graffiti on the walls. A couple of friends have made the trip out to see me so I wander between them and the dressing room, trying to look purposeful as I cross the stage, but really having nowhere to go and nothing to do.

Tonight I try something different and start with a quiet song called 'The Kingdom'. In 2012, I created the music for a new play that layered the Oedipus myth with Irish

161

migrant workers building the motorway tunnels of England. One of the actors was also a stand-up comedian who kept us entertained in rehearsals. He kept saying he had written some lyrics inspired by the play and wanted me to set them to music. Because he was a comedian I thought it was going to be a funny song, but what he gave me were beautiful words steeped in elegant images. When I sat down with a guitar the music tumbled out. Close up to the microphone, I sing in a whisper that Mark lifts to match the volume of the guitar and people stop talking and listen.

There is a small but appreciative audience on each side of the stage, others cluster fifteen feet away and there is a big empty space in front of me, but enough people are listening to make the applause sound positive. As I play, more people arrive, and the noise from the bar increases. Up until now I have been in control, with the hyperawareness of the last two performances mercifully absent. So I am taken by surprise when I begin a song and know something is going wrong, but cannot work out what it can be. The song, called 'Wild Nights', was written twenty years ago and has been revived at the suggestion of my son, who remembers me singing the chorus – I didn't know it all the way through – when he was young. Tonight, it seems as if the frets are in the wrong place and when I start to sing my voice feels absurdly low. While I outwardly perform, my inner self tries to work out what is going on. Halfway through I spot the capo is missing and I am singing in the wrong key.

My half hour passes quickly, then I bow down low and wave to the crowd, feeling a little like the rock and roll singer I wanted to be when I was fifteen. I feel considerably less rock and roll half an hour later when the next act comes on. T-Toe is a man who sings, raps, plays the trombone and drinks multiple pints on stage during his set. One number consists of him bending over, pointing at his bum and screaming, 'Fuck my anus,' over a backing track. The audience in the Thunderbolt absolutely love it.

Then Kid Carpet comes on and the whole place goes crazy. Dave serves my free pint of lager and I stand where there was an empty space during my set. Now it is packed with Carpet fans and I raise my arm to sway from side to side along with them, as we all sing the chorus from 'Jesus is a Hedgehog', one of the many catchy tunes that keep everyone leaping, dancing and singing for the next hour.

In the morning I am up early and cycle to the University of the West of England, where I am playing various witnesses in a mock trial for student barristers, one of the odd jobs I have taken on to keep the money coming in. The sky is bright and there is an intimation of spring in the cold air. I feel different and it takes a while to work out why. Then I get it. Cycling along the backroads of Bristol this morning I feel truly alive. I used to think that playing music would be a more intense version of listening to it. I know now that is not the case, as there are too many things going on, too much to think about. But last night I was not hiding behind anyone else and I was not standing in the shadows. I might have been bottom of the bill, but I was authentically, properly me. And the sensation of being alive after playing a gig is truly, wonderfully, amazing.

If Everyone Was Listening, 1977

It is a Friday evening in June and the night of our first proper gig. The church on the hill has a youth club and we are playing at the summer disco in the Canon Newman Hall. We recruited our parents to ferry our equipment and now here we are setting up on the floor in the corner. The man who runs the youth club is watching us and looking a bit agitated, rubbing the bald patch on his head. They have never had a group play here before and are worried what will happen. I got us this gig; I just walked in one Friday night and asked. The youth club man was worried we were a punk group and I had to assure him we most certainly were not.

'When you've set up I'm going to go for a walk to see how far the sound travels,' the man tells us. 'If it's too loud you're going to have to turn it down. No arguments, please.'

Andy looks disgusted. 'I can't turn down the drums.'

'No, but you can play them quietly. Use brushes or something,' the man says, turning his back on us and walking into the kitchen where Coke, lemonade and plates of crisps are being readied.

'I don't do brushes, man,' says Andy, under his breath.

The evening sun is streaming through the large windows of the hall. Andy adjusts his drums, Fred fiddles with his amplifier and Matthew prowls like a tiger. As the bass player I am not the centre of attention and discover this also means I am not as nervous as when we played at Whitegates. But – and this is beginning to seem like an advantage – I still get to have all the fun. Close by, our friend Barry plugs in his mobile disco. We are learning fast and have discovered the singing needs to go through a different set of speakers to the guitars or you can't hear it properly. Barry is letting us use his, but insists they are positioned either side of his record decks, rather than either side of us.

Fred decides everything is ready. 'Let's run through a couple of numbers,' he says. We start to play the Santana song 'Black Magic Woman' to the empty hall. A few minutes later the youth club man comes rushing through the door, waving his arms.

'I can hear it all the way to the top of Church Hill,' he tells us. 'You're going to have to turn it right down.'

'OK,' we say, 'leave it with us.' We move to our amplifiers and make a show of turning them down while hardly moving the knobs at all.

'You'll all be deaf by the time you're forty,' he calls to us, going back to the kitchen again. We all laugh at this. Being forty is so far off it is impossible to imagine. And deaf? What does he know?

People start arriving and the curtains are closed. The late sun floods through the gaps and columns of dust swirl and dance in shafts of light. Groups of girls cluster together on one side of the hall holding bottles of Coke, while boys do the same on the other side. They exchange furtive glances with each other. When Barry puts on the latest record by Abba all the girls rush to the middle of the floor and start dancing in small closed circles. A couple of the more confident boys start dancing by themselves, not moving their bodies very much, working their way into the circles, then picking off a girl to dance with. No one is making eye contact with anyone else. Most of the other boys stay on the sides watching and making little twitching movements with their legs.

This goes on for ages.

Then it is time.

I strap on the bass; Andy sits behind his drums and adjusts them again; Fred kneels down by his amplifier; Matthew picks up the microphone and looks down at the floor. As soon as the record finishes lots of people disappear through the doors to go outside, so the crowd on the dance floor is small and those who are left form a polite semicircle around us. Barry starts speaking into his microphone. 'Let's hear a big Hythe Youth Club welcome for the Entangled Network.' Then Fred counts us in and we start to play.

Swinging the bass to the rhythm of the music, I dip the neck towards the floor and then up again in exaggerated, sweeping movements. I am determined not to disappear into the background and stand forward to jerk and thrust the guitar towards the crowd: I want to be seen tonight. To begin with everyone stands rigid, glued to the spot. Then, one of the confident boys moves out of the semicircle and nods his head to the beat. A few others follow, hands wedged firmly into front trouser pockets. There are not many girls watching and those that do are squinting at us, not sure what to make of it yet. I notice they do not nod their heads, tap their feet or respond to the music at all. At the very back of the crowd I see the head of the youth club leader bobbing about. 'Too loud,' he mouths. We ignore him.

We play 'Black Magic Woman' and then 'Helpless'. We have rehearsed the actual songs but have not practised how to get from one song to another. The bands I have seen end a number, shout a quick introduction then begin the next. When we end a song there is a long gap, during which Fred tunes up and Andy and I make noises with the bass and drums. Over the top of this racket Matthew tries to talk. After 'Johnny B. Goode', Fred takes off his electric guitar, leans it against the amplifier and sits at the upright piano. We are going to play our version of the Supertramp song 'If Everyone Was Listening'. Being able to say we play songs with a piano was how I proved to the youth club leader we were not a punk band. Fred has arranged the song so he accompanies Matthew on his own during the verses before Andy and I come crashing in with the bass and drums at the start of the chorus. This gives me a chance to practise something I have seen musicians doing at the Leas Cliff Hall and have become rather good at, which is standing on stage and not doing anything at all, while making it clear to the audience I am waiting for my moment. I do this by closing my eyes and swaying to the music, opening them every now and then to glance at Andy who is doing the same. If we open our eyes at the same time we share a conspiratorial smile. Occasionally I will perform a mock run down my fretboard while Andy plays mime drum rolls in advance of our cue.

'Thank you very much,' says Matthew. 'This next one's written by Paul. It's called "Dissolution".' I might not be singing or playing the guitar, but I can make an impact writing songs. I had a copy of *Roget's Thesaurus* for Christmas and it came into its own one wet Sunday afternoon, when I hid in my bedroom to emerge hours later with the lyrics for 'Dissolution'. I take a little bow at the end of the song.

The more we play the more the shape of the semicircle is less defined. There is not exactly dancing going on, but a few of the girls are now tapping their feet to the rhythm. The last number is 'Wild Thing'. My guitar lead is long enough for me to run up and down, bend down low and then jump into the air. I look out at the nodding heads and imagine I am looking into a mighty crowd, hair flying like spray on the wild, stormy English Channel.

At the end, I want us all to stand in front of the drums, put our arms around each other's shoulders and take a bow together, like I have seen bands do on the TV, but before I can organise this Barry puts on a disco record. The doors at the back of the hall open and everyone outside comes back in. The floor is full in moments and everyone is dancing.

Video Killed the Radio Star, 2016

Despite timing everything carefully, I leave late, get stuck in traffic on the Portway and have to warm up my voice in the car, as I drive to dBs Music in the centre of Bristol, where my friend Tom runs a filmmaking school. I have been scouring the internet and it seems as though every singer-songwriter has decent footage of themselves in action. As useful as it is to have sound recordings online, I need some live videos as well, so Tom has come to my aid and arranged for his degree students to record four songs. In my quest for authenticity I am wearing the same clothes I have been in all day, a thick blue jumper and an old pair of jeans.

Parking on a side street I look up at tall cranes stretching into the sky, ropes trailing from their jibs and swinging in the wind. The film studios are in another part of town where the cityscape is changing fast and redundant industrial buildings are being torn down and replaced by blocks of flats with street-level coffee shops. Tom meets me on the step and gives me a tour of the building. They have only just moved in and the whole place smells of new carpets, fresh paint and computers. We go into the studio where several students are ready to go, each in charge of a camera. Beyond a window is the sound cubicle where another student sits at a digital desk. They treat me as though I am a proper visiting artist and in response I try to appear as if I do this sort of thing all the time and it is no big deal.

Perching on a stool I play through 'Poppysong' while the students listen politely and applaud at the end. Then I play it over and over again while sound levels are set and the cameras are adjusted. All the time this is a rehearsal I am perfectly relaxed and make no mistakes. Once everyone is happy and we go for a take, my throat tightens, suddenly aware of the performance. What should I be looking at? Should I stare at the cameras as if they were an imaginary audience? There are several of them and all are recording for editing later, so the chances are I would be looking at the wrong one. I don't want to shut my eyes because that looks terrible on camera, so focus on the microphone in front of me. There is a silence in a studio that is different to any other as the walls are acoustically treated to absorb sound, with very little reflected back to the ears. Halfway through 'Poppysong' I start thinking about the silence, then the thought takes over and I make a mistake. I start again and make another mistake, so we decide to try another song and come back to this one later. I have just begun to play when the haze machine – a device putting a fine mist in the air to soften the light and my appearance on camera – causes the fire alarm to go off and we all troop outside. When we get back I pull myself together and do the song in one take. Then we run through the others and by eight o'clock we are finished. As the cameras are packed away I sit in the sound cubicle and listen back. My voice and guitar have been recorded well and I hear subtleties of breath and harmonic detail in the big studio speakers. With guitar case in hand I walk out and past the Fleece and Firkin – one of Bristol's most popular music venues – where the audience for tonight's gig are spilling onto benches outside, allowing a trickle of excitement that at last I am part of the same world.

Breaking Up Is Hard to Do, 1977

The morning after the gig I go to work in the jewellery shop. Before I leave the house I put on my aviator sunglasses and walk through the allotments like a rock star. All weekend I am scheming, so by the time we meet again in the Whitegates day room I can't wait to tell the band what we should do next. I explain there are youth clubs out on the Romney Marsh in Dymchurch, New Romney and Lydd as well as the nearby villages of Elham, Lyminge and Stelling Minnis. I imagine us playing all of them, getting better and better until, sitting in the back of our parents' cars, we ride in to Folkestone like conquering heroes. Andy shares my excitement, but Fred and Matthew are not looking at each other. This had been going on before the gig but I thought the thrill of actually performing would bring us together. Suddenly, it blows up and they are shouting at each other. I am facing the other way and without looking turn with the bass around my neck. Matthew is standing in the way and the headstock hits him in the face with a horrible thud. He falls to the floor, then gets up and calmly walks out of the room and away from the Entangled Network.

The three of us stand in silence looking at the door. Then we look out of the window. It is a sunny evening and there is a game of football going on in the park outside. There are boys I recognise from school and I watch them running, laughing and having fun. I want to find a way to suggest I could be the singer, when Fred starts talking. 'Actually, there's something I want to say.' I have such a bad feeling about what is coming I start to talk, not giving Fred a chance to speak, hoping that if I say enough, he'll be distracted and whatever it is will remain unsaid.

'I think we should be heavier because the heavier stuff seemed to go down well,' I say. 'I think we should get T-shirts printed; I think we should tape the letters EN on the bass drum so we look more professional.' Idea after idea pours out of my mouth without pause. But Fred silences me by shaking his head.

'I've been asked to join another group,' he tells us. 'They're older guys. Jazz rock.'

In the silence that follows I hear the muffled sound of bell-ringing practice from the church on the hill. 'Couldn't you be in that group as well as ours?' says Andy.

'Not really,' replies Fred. 'They've got gigs lined up. Wouldn't be time.'

'Gigs?' I say. 'Where?'

'First one's at the Phoenix Tea Rooms.' Fred looks a bit sheepish.

'That's in Folkestone,' I say, trying to control my voice and not show the hurt.

'I know,' says Fred. 'Sorry.'

Andy is shaking his head. 'I don't get it, Fred. Why them?'

Fred stares at the floor for what seems like ages then looks into the middle distance. 'I guess they're… well… proper musicians.'

Then Fred puts the black Fender Stratocaster back in the case, snaps the lid shut, fastens each of the catches and walks away from the band, leaving me with the bass guitar around my neck and Andy sitting behind the drum kit.

I look out of the day-room windows to the park. The boys are still playing football without a care in the world and the bells are ringing in the church on the hill.

It feels like the dream is over.

Keep Yourself Alive, 2016

The sleeplessness returns on Wednesday. This is because on Saturday afternoon I have a slot at the Porthleven Food Festival, when a little Cornish port turns into a giant party with a live soundtrack. This time I will be performing for a whole hour, so it is a big step from all that has gone before. On Friday night I manage just three hours' sleep, but am getting so used to anxiety ramping up before a show it feels almost normal. Sarah arrives early on Saturday to pick me up and as we drive onto the motorway I talk rapidly and randomly, afraid that silence will allow fear to creep in. We stop at a café near Oakhampton but all I want is a takeaway tea and a single digestive biscuit. I have added spoken word sections to my set now, telling musical stories from childhood, and try them out on Sarah as we drive. When she laughs, the tension eases and I start to look forward to the afternoon, enjoying the open road and big skies over Devon. The sun comes out as we head west into Cornwall and the satnav guides us all the way to the centre of Porthleven. Today, the village is packed with crowds, music and the smell of cooking, all brightly lit by cold spring sunshine. We find the stage, with my name written on a chalk board outside. The venue seats about 100 people and has a bar at the back. There are a couple of hours before the show and I am suddenly hungry, so we meander through the crowds and sit on the harbour wall where I force down a vegetable burrito. In my pre-show state of mind, everything is heightened as though normality is intensified. The light on the water seems vivid; the surging crowds are full of vibrant colours; the air is rich with the smell of sea infused with the aroma of food. We walk out of the village and watch waves roll along the harbour wall and see surfers riding breakers up the coast. I collect the gear from the car and walk towards the tent, waiting outside as chef Antony Worrall Thompson finishes his talk. There is half an hour to go. The sound guy says hello and I run through a few songs on stage. When I begin, the tent is about half full and I look out to Cornish friends smiling encouragingly. As I start to sing 'The Kingdom', I realise how many things I can see. Within my line of vision people wander in, tune in for a moment and wander out; someone right in front of me stares at his phone and swipes as if he's on Tinder looking for a date; there are conversations going on; a woman in a large hat and summer dress slowly works her way through a complicated meal on a cardboard tray.

I don't notice the boatbuilder at first. There are so many things going on, and so much extraneous noise, I think the sound of woodworking must be coming from a display outside the tent. Then, during 'Poppysong', I look to my right and see a man a few feet away with a wood plane, who is actually in the middle of building a wooden boat, right here, next to me in the marquee. He is part of a display I hadn't noticed before. Once I see him, I cannot get his rhythm out of my head, even though it is working against the song I am singing. I try to turn it into a joke, hoping he will stop, but he just smiles and carries on.

Despite the boatbuilder pulling focus away from the stage, everything is going well. The songs are getting plenty of applause and the spoken word sections get laughs in the right places. Then music starts up outside and I suddenly feel as though I have a disco in my head. The sound guy goes off to get the music turned down and then takes the opportunity to have a cigarette in the sunshine. I see him standing there at the very moment I need the microphone for the shruti box to be faded up. Because I cannot get his attention, I hold the instrument by my head where it will be picked up by the vocal mic, but the sound is so loud in my ear I am unable to pitch the first line of 'Coal Not Dole' so it is hopelessly off-key. I find my way back and carry on and at this point realise I am enjoying it, really enjoying this gig. During the final song, two girls walk in, listen to the music for a moment, then dance across the tent to the bar, buy drinks, then dance back out again. Then it is all over, people clap and I am handed a pint of lager. There is, I realise, nothing so good as the taste of chilled beer after a show. Outside in cold sunshine I talk to friends and former students. Sarah and I eat fish and chips in the village then drive through the dusk to our hotel on The Lizard. The feeling of aliveness infuses me again and lingers all the way back to Bristol the next day.

God Save the Queen, 1977

The week after the gig at the youth club, on the day of the Queen's Silver Jubilee, Andy and I take the bus to Folkestone to watch a band playing covers of early Beatles songs at an afternoon concert in the Leas Cliff Hall. It is sparsely attended and the curtains have been left open, so we sit on the balcony and stare despondently at where bright sun is reflecting off the sea.

Meanwhile, seventy miles away in London, the Sex Pistols have chartered a boat and are sailing down the Thames playing 'God Save the Queen', a song that has been banned from the radio but still reaches number two in the charts. This afternoon, watching the group in their Beatle suits singing a pale imitation of 'Love Me Do', I feel as far away from where things are actually happening as it is possible to be.

Another Nail in My Heart, 2016

One afternoon in late April, I am at home in the living room ten minutes before I leave to catch the train to an important meeting. I look at the middle finger of my right hand and see a split nail. I need long nails on my right hand to pick the guitar strings and the pressure of constant playing means they often break. A single broken nail means an uneven sound, but worse, if one of the strings is played with the soft pad of a finger it will blister and make it hard to play anything at all. If I ignore the tear I will lose the nail, but if I try a repair I risk missing the train. With gigs coming up, including a headline show in a theatre, I dare not risk a full break, so reach for the superglue. There are various nail-hardening oils available, but after consulting online forums, I have decided superglue is the best option. Already seven minutes have passed. I undo the lid and dip the brush in the liquid, then carefully coat each nail, paying special attention to the one with the split. Then, Suzy Soot, my very fluffy black cat, leaps on to the desk and tries to nuzzle the brush hand. I restrain him. It is now past leaving time, so I sweep the cat off the desk, put the lid on the glue tube and run. Crossing the footbridge over the River Trym, a comfortable two-minute walk from the station, I hear the train approaching, so the run becomes a sprint and I throw myself on board just as the doors are shutting. When the conductor comes to sell me a ticket, she suggests leaving home a little earlier, stopping mid-sentence to stare at my right hand. I look too and see long strands of black hair coming from the end of each finger, so my hand looks like a Troll Doll from the 1970s. I try to explain that my cat got in the way while I was doing my nails. The conductor raises her eyebrows and walks down the carriage in silence.

Blue Suede Shoes, 1977

Now it is the summer holiday and Mum and Dad decide we will go to the Devon Coast Country Club with Cousin Nick and family, where we will be given our own basic room, some distance away from their en-suite accommodation. The Devon Coast Country Club looks a lot like a holiday camp to me, with rows of chalets and organised fun, but if I ever say this out loud Mum gets cross. 'It is not a holiday camp, it is a country club,' she says. I take my guitar with me, and one day we are sitting outside on the grass, working through the songs I know, when a boy about my age walks past. He stops to talk and tells us he is a drummer and has just been recruited to play in the house band this evening, as their drummer left unexpectedly. He asks if I play the bass, as their bass player has gone too. When I say I do, he goes off for a few minutes, returning with the news that I am now a member of the band and should report for duty this evening at eight.

I don't get worried at first as I have no idea what's going to happen, but later that evening, standing in a dimly lit backstage corridor, with a borrowed bass around my neck, I wonder what I have got myself into. The band is led by Jim the keyboard player – permed hair and flared trousers – who shakes my hand and says, 'We're doing standards so follow me. All right?'

'That's good for me,' I say confidently, knowing there is little hope I will actually be able to follow what the keyboard player is doing by watching his hands or hearing him play. I am just not good enough to do that. The compère, all sideburns and blue velvet jacket, is in the corridor too and a couple of girls slip through the curtain from the main hall to see him. He cuddles each one then whispers something in their ears. They giggle and kiss him on the cheek, then slip back into the hall. It all feels a little bit like what rock and roll should be, but not quite. Then we are on stage and looking through bright stage lights to where the crowd are dim silhouettes on the balconies above. A few middle-aged couples have come out in front and are ready to dance.

'"Blue Suede Shoes" in F,' says Jim, who counts us in. The Elvis song is an easy twelve-bar blues and I am able to add a few fancy finger slides that make Jim smile and nod in my direction, so at the end I get a special round of applause. After that it goes downhill. 'American Patrol' in E-flat is next and when it becomes clear I cannot follow his hands on the keyboard, Jim calls out the chords. The problem is there are so many of them and they change so fast I can't detect a pattern. Eventually Jim stops calling out the chords, so I turn down the volume on the bass and just pretend to play for the rest of the set. Afterwards the drummer is offered a job with the band for the rest of the season while I get a pat on the shoulder and a sympathetic smile. Jim says he will buy me a drink in the bar but after an hour I realise he is not going to show up. Out of the window I see the two girls who had been in the corridor walking towards the accommodation section and disappearing behind a door that says 'Staff Only'.

Hal-an-Tow, 2016

I am sitting in the kitchen rehearsing for a lunchtime show on the forthcoming bank holiday weekend and get two-thirds of the way through 'Brislington Diamonds' before breaking into a cough. This has started to happen more and more. Constant singing over the last few months has put a strain on my vocal cords, so I buy honey-and-ginger teabags and scour the internet for advice. I conclude I am not warming up and not breathing properly.

This time the performance anxiety doesn't kick in until the day before, but when it arrives it is pretty ferocious and I wander around the house in the early hours making tea and waiting for the dawn.

The gig is at the Bell Inn, a music pub on Walcot Street in Bath, where a friend has organised an event in aid of cancer charities. I am on a bill with a few other singers and only have to play four songs. It is my last chance to practise in the company of others before holding the stage on my own. There is no soundcheck as such and the gig is a bit shambolic, which suits me well. Two other performers go first and I sit watching with a mug of honey-and-ginger tea, before I am introduced and launch into 'Brislington Diamonds'. The stage faces a wall with an archway that leads to a small room taken up with a pool table, so most of the audience are to my left and right and I swivel my head like an owl to see them. I follow 'Brislington Diamonds' with an old folk song, 'Spencer the Rover', which starts well. Halfway through, Spencer spends a night in the woods lamenting the family he abandoned and decides to return home. I have devised a little guitar motif here that divides the song in two and involves moving up the fretboard to pick a simple riff. During the microsecond my hand travels upward I realise I have forgotten where I should stop, so pick a fret at random. The riff that follows is a confusion of wrong notes but this gets a big laugh and a cheer. When I do it again at the end – I still can't remember where to stop – the cheer is repeated. I realise if you make mistakes in the right way, they get big laughs.

In 1990 I had a job in a department of the BBC World Service called – with echoes of a bygone age – the Pop Music Unit. One of the programmes I had to produce was called *Folk in Britain*. Knowing very little about folk music, the presenter sent me away to listen to a band who combined the energy of punk rock with traditional folk. 'Hal-an-Tow' was the first song I heard by the Oysterband and I was hooked, as what they were doing with English folk tunes was similar to the way the Pogues had energised Irish music. It is a song that celebrates the turning year; a version is sung in the Cornish town of Helston at the Flora Day festival and I have heard it sung, late afternoon on May Day, in a pub in Brighton by a band of weary morris men who had danced since dawn. As my gig at the Bell Inn was on 1 May, it seemed the perfect song to end the set.

To play 'Hal-an-Tow' I retune the guitar, a skill I had continued to practise at home. The process takes a couple of minutes during which I must not ignore the audience or attention will be lost, so I carry on talking while twisting the tuning pegs. I discover I can do this as long as I talk about tuning. If I venture onto something else, both tuning and the talking go wrong. As this discovery is made live with me narrating it, I get a laugh and everyone seems to be on my side. I swivel my owl head and ask both ends of the audience to stomp along to 'Hal-an-Tow', and almost everyone joins in, so human percussion underpins the whole song. Playing the final chord I jump in the air. As I land I see a man in a brown leather jacket gripping a pint with one hand and pumping his fist in the air with the other.

Helpless, 1977

Andy and I reconvene in the day room. Because I do not have an electric guitar, I use my acoustic with a huge pickup inserted in the soundhole and feed that and the vocal microphone into our one small amplifier. It isn't very loud so the drums frequently drown out everything else. I have been busy writing songs and one includes the line, 'It's a pity she's a whore, 'cos I ain't got no money no more.' It is glaringly obvious we are not a band any more.

At school we hear of a boy in the third year who owns a bass guitar and amplifier. Being fifteen, we wouldn't normally go near a thirteen-year-old, but he has a bass and we need him. It takes quite a bit of doing but eventually we persuade Paul into the day room for a rehearsal. He might only be thirteen but with his black curly hair and check shirt he looks good, which is a start. Paul has just been given the instrument and doesn't know how to play it yet. We run through 'Helpless' – a three-chord song by Neil Young – and I show Paul the three notes he needs to play. He finds this difficult and drifts out of time. We stick with him as he looks cool and we don't have any other choice. When he comes to rehearsals Paul concentrates so hard I can imagine what he will be like in a few months' time. After all it was not so long ago Andy and I were in the same place. Paul is a comfortable presence and before long we are a band again.

Perfectly Good Guitar, 2016

One afternoon I kneel at the foot of my bed and peer at the mess swept underneath: books, magazines, newspapers and a crate of shampoo bottles pilfered from hotel rooms. From further back I pull out a bodhrán. It's coated in dust and I scrape off a lump of solidified cat sick. I lie on the floor and crawl under the bed to pull out a guitar case. The dust is thick all over but when I flick the catches it is like opening an oyster shell to reveal a pearl. Inside is my old electric guitar, saved up for and bought with my dad in 1977. It was loved but has been unplayed for years. Now I am all acoustic, I have decided to give the guitar to my son.

Can't Make Up My Mind, 1977

It is a weekday in half term and I am at Sandling station with my life savings and my dad. He has taken a day off work to come to London and supervise my purchase of an electric guitar. Standing on the platform and looking down the line for the train to appear from the tunnel, I feel inside my wallet to touch the notes, crisp from the bank and warm from my pocket. There is a total of £135 and it is all the money I have in the world, earned from my Saturday job, a paper round and Christmas and birthday presents too.

Things have changed at home. Mum and Dad occasionally buy pop records themselves, though not anything cool enough for me to enjoy. When their friends come for dinner it is not unusual to find them, late in the evening, dancing like beanpoles to the sounds of Abba or the Carpenters. They are also tolerating my growing obsession with rock music and, one morning, actually seem interested when I dominate the conversation at breakfast with a long speech about the merits of a guitar riff in a Led Zeppelin record. Crucially, they are prepared to drive us around, picking up and delivering equipment and taking us to and from gigs. And Dad wants to know all about my new guitar.

We are slightly awkward with each other at first, because I am nervous about spending my money and do not want to admit this to him. He smokes a cigarette, stubs it out with his foot and kicks the butt onto the tracks.

'Have you got a shortlist?' he asks, once we are on the train. I think I have but am not sure. 'You should make a list of the advantages and the disadvantages of each one,' he tells me. I have seen Dad do this at home when he has to decide something, like which lawnmower to buy. He draws two columns side by side and titles and underlines them Advantages and Disadvantages. He then makes lists under each heading. Dad is so logical the right answer is obvious. When I try the exercise, both columns end up with the same number of points and I am even more confused.

'I just can't make up my mind, Dad,' I say. 'Maybe it'll be easier when I see them.' I look through the window as the fields of Kent turn into dirty grey suburbs of South London.

We get off the train and thread our way through crowds on the Charing Cross Road. I feel slightly sick. There is only one chance to get this right; it would take a lifetime to save this much money again. There is a hierarchy to guitar ownership. If you are a proper musician you buy one made by Gibson or Fender, like the Stratocaster Fred owns, but these are way out of my budget and would take years of saving. The trick, I have decided, is to buy a guitar that does not make me feel like second best. Lots of electric guitars are copies of Gibson and Fender instruments, but just seem cheap and nasty. I want people to look at my guitar and think I am a proper musician. Up until now there has been luscious pleasure in weighing up the possibilities, but now I have to make a decision.

We walk into a music shop on Denmark Street. It is dark with a forest of guitars on the floor and others hanging suspended from the ceiling. The salesman has long hair, a scruffy T-shirt and looks like a roadie at the Leas Cliff Hall. He asks my budget, I tell him and he purses his lips and breathes in through his teeth. He goes to the back of the shop and comes back with a copy of a Fender Telecaster. 'This axe is pretty cool for the price, man.' He has a hippy drawl and I can see it is making Dad uncomfortable.

'What does axe mean?' he says quietly when the salesman goes off to find a lead. He comes back and plugs me in. I play a few notes. The amplifier is turned up so loud it makes everything in the shop rattle.

'Yeah, man. Go for it. Make some noise,' says the salesman. But I am too self-conscious to go for it, feel out of my depth and the guitar he has given me doesn't feel very nice. Shuffling uncomfortably from foot to foot, Dad looks like a visitor from another planet in his green anorak and Marks & Spencer trousers. So we leave and walk through Chinatown to Chappell's in Bond Street. Here the atmosphere is completely different. Everything is neat and tidy and the salesman, wearing a suit this time, hands me a guitar called an Ibanez PF100. Although this is a copy of a Gibson Les Paul, it has the weight and feel of the real thing. The body has a sunburst finish that catches the light and even Dad is impressed.

'That looks like it's well made. Good construction; solid parts; well-polished wood.' I plug in the guitar and the salesman leaves me to play blues riffs, while I try to catch my reflection in the window to see what I look like. Most importantly, I do not feel like second best. Then the salesman returns with a hard case lined with bright orange fake fur and that is what decides it, because just as much as the guitar, a hard case will make me look like a proper musician. When I hand over my money I am still feeling sick.

Look at us walking back to Charing Cross through Soho, me holding the guitar at my side and wondering if people think I am a rock star, rather than a teenage boy out with his dad. I am fifteen years old and do not know how rare and precious it is to spend a whole day with my father and for him to be interested enough to take a day off work and come all the way to London in pursuit of my dream.

From Me to You, 2016

My son Fred's musical adventures began two years ago, when I spent a Saturday morning tramping around the music shops of Bristol in search of a guitar for his birthday. Beginners usually start with nylon strings because they are kinder to the fingers, but I decided Fred was best with a steel strung acoustic, so he would be closer to making the sound he could hear in his head. I remembered my frustration, thrashing a cheap classical guitar in my bedroom. For a couple of months Fred's guitar sat in the corner of his room. I was not patient and struggled to teach basic chords. Then he started watching YouTube videos and found better guidance in the virtual world. Fred's hands suffered for a few weeks until the pads on his fingers hardened, and by then he was as obsessed as I had been forty years before. Now he is ready to go electric.

In the bedroom I strum a chord on my old Ibanez PF100, which is hopelessly out of tune on ten-year-old strings, but the weight of the guitar makes me think of the day I first held it. Dad would love to know the instrument was going to his grandson and be excited this is the start of another musical adventure. I take the guitar to the shop that fixed my broken Martin and it comes back with bright strings and the body polished and shining. I give Fred a small amplifier too and we sit together as he discovers the possibilities of electric music. I play a slow blues progression on his acoustic guitar while he picks a solo over the top, exploring the wild, unpredictable excitement of distorted sound. I recognise the feeling from four decades back.

Every Day is a Winding Road, 2016

Arriving in Penzance with an incredibly heavy bag on wheels and a guitar, I walk out of the station and blink in bright Cornish sunlight. I am on my way to the Isles of Scilly to play at the Old Town Inn on Saturday night, a journey that involves two days' travel by train and ship. There will be no support act and I am not supporting anyone else; it will be just me. I cannot fly on the little plane as the guitar, shruti box, tuners, wires and cases weigh far too much. I wheel the weighty bag through the streets and check into a neat little B&B in a side street, where a small terraced house has been carved into multiple en-suite bedrooms. The proprietor greets me with a sheen of friendly professionalism and a heavy German accent, telling me to leave both bag and guitar in the breakfast room as my bedroom is so small. He asks what time I want breakfast, what I would like for breakfast, coffee or tea, whether the toast should be brown or white, marmalade or jam?

I meet a friend who has driven from Falmouth and we go for dinner. She parks near the B&B and before going home needs the loo, so I offer the micro-cubicle in my room. We are halfway up the stairs when the proprietor bursts out of his quarters.

'What do you think you're doing?' he says, voice loaded with barely suppressed rage. I explain my friend wants to use the toilet. He quivers and then explodes: 'Guests are not allowed in the rooms.'

'She just wants to use the toilet,' I repeat.

His face turns bright red and he starts to shout. 'You will disturb all the other guests. How dare you. How dare you.' She uses the loo anyway then creeps down the stairs and drives home. I go to sleep wondering if Bob Dylan has to put up with this sort of thing.

The proprietor apologises for his outburst at breakfast and then again when I leave. 'We'll say no more about it,' he says as I crane the bag into the boot of a taxi.

It is a beautiful morning under a sapphire sky. I put my bags inside the ship then come out on deck to watch shimmering water, the green line of Cornish clifftops and the slight swell as we pass Land's End and head into the Atlantic. When the ship sails into Scilly waters the colour of the sea is turquoise. We pass between the islands of St Mary's and St Agnes and I see the familiar shapes of Samson, Bryher and Tresco.

It is good to be back at Carnwethers, although all is chaos, as the kitchen is in the middle of redecoration and a hot water tank is being replaced. Louise – co-owner and manager who is letting me stay for nothing – puts down her paintbrushes and makes me a cup of tea, before I record a session on Radio Scilly.

A friend organised the whole weekend and I sent her a pack of flyers in the post. As we drive towards the radio station my picture is on every noticeboard. The great thing about playing on a small island, I realise, is the ease of getting the word out, unlike in a city, where tweets, flyers and posters disappear in a blizzard of competition. Radio Scilly is based on the floor above an estate agent just outside Hugh Town. There is a large studio, a small office, one full-time employee and lots of community volunteers. The station's new full-time broadcaster is a young guy called Will. When I started speaking on the radio, the advice I was given was to be like myself but 20 per cent more. Will must have been given similar advice but with a greater percentage, maybe 80 per cent. It works though as I am sleepy and he wakes me up. We record a twenty-minute interview, I play two songs and it all feels perfectly normal. Then I walk out of the studio and straight on to the beach.

Now I'm busy, performance anxiety drops into the background. It is still with me when I wake up in the night, but nothing like the overwhelming force that ruled my life a few gigs ago.

Early on Friday morning, I run a big circuit on empty roads to the music of birdsong. When I get back I repair another split nail with superglue, then sit in the conservatory – the location of the party three years ago – and sing, as

Louise works through a mountain of ironing. She applauds after each song and even tells me I have a *good voice*. This is the first time anyone has ever said this, so I go straight upstairs and mark the occasion with an entry in my diary. Then we gather among the paintbrushes in the kitchen and listen to my interview on Radio Scilly. With the posters, the interview and the rehearsal, it feels as if, at last, this whole adventure is gathering momentum.

That afternoon I take the community bus to the Old Town Inn so I can look at the venue and talk to the landlord. The stonework outside makes the pub look older than it is, so I am surprised to walk into a large open-plan bar with a high ceiling and low stage in the far corner. Paul, the landlord, shows me around and I spot folding dividers that turn the stage into a rectangular, club-like zone, sealed off from the rest of the bar. In situations like this I am always keen to please, so when Paul says the dividers will stay open and the tables set for dinner I nod my head and smile, even though all instincts are screaming, 'Shut the dividers and don't let anyone eat in front of me.' I do speak up though when Paul says he will leave an open space in front of the stage in case anyone wants to dance. 'I don't think they will,' I say. Paul shows me the PA system, which he says I can use even though it belongs to the folk club. There are a lot of wires and I wonder where they all go.

On Saturday evening I take a taxi to the Old Town Inn for six o'clock. It has been a busy day; I've led a writing workshop, drunk loads of tea and not had enough to eat. Paul and I stand in front of a pile of equipment. He sets the speakers on stands but doesn't know how to make the PA system work, so I piece it together like a jigsaw puzzle, though I can't figure out how to connect the sound desk, and hope there will be enough volume in the speakers themselves to cut through the noise of people talking.

The pub has been open all day and a few customers have been drinking for hours. An extremely drunk man staggers over and asks me to call his mate with a 'brilliant voice' on stage to sing. I politely tell him to go away, which he does for five minutes before coming back and asking the same thing again. There are rectangular dinner tables set all around and I feel a bit like the act at a 1970s dinner dance, rather than the artsy, urban folk musician I would like to be. By now Paul has disappeared, so I requisition a tourist to help me soundcheck, which he does with enthusiasm, moving around the bar to listen while texting his daughter to say he has become a sound engineer.

When people I know start to arrive I go for a walk to Old Town beach and hide myself away for half an hour, shivering in shirtsleeves, looking out at swirling sea fret. I have barely eaten anything all day and the feeling suddenly hits me: I am incredibly, ravenously hungry. Paul offered me food from the bar menu when I arrived and I turned it down, being too anxious to tackle a pub meal, but now all I can think about are two bananas in my bag on the side of the stage. The pub is full of people and I devour both bananas, drink water and slither around the room, trying not to engage in complicated conversations.

At 8:30 I walk on to the stage. There are a lot of people out there, but because many are sitting at tables the audience is thinly spread around the pub, with concentrations at the extremities where there are bench seats. As the stage is in a corner, some of the audience are just out of sight. I start with 'Pelistry', an instrumental I named after a bay on St Mary's, and it gets a big cheer at the end. After retuning one string I play 'Hal-an-Tow' and manage to get half the audience clapping along. Then two things happen at once: the hunger returns with a vengeance and I become obsessed with three people at the table nearest the stage.

There is a woman watching me intensely, and two men dressed in navy blue, one of whom has a spectacular beard like the captain of a ship. They are in the middle of eating dinner. Just before I went on stage someone had mentioned these people were from the folk club and at the time I had thought no more about it. Now, as I am singing, my inner self goes on a strange journey. I wonder if Paul asked if we could borrow the PA, so maybe they are furious that I turned up and used it without permission and are sitting right at the front to make a point. Maybe they are highly skilled folk musicians who are appalled by my lack of professionalism and will stand up and declare me an imposter. This is made worse when I invite audience participation and the woman claps along but the sea captain stares at me without moving his hands. When I talk to the crowd and look at him, he offers nothing back. Meanwhile the hunger is making it hard to concentrate on anything at all apart from the contents of the fridge at Carnwethers.

I have a row of domestic spotlights aimed at my face, so cannot see far into the crowd, but despite the hunger and rising paranoia, I get the feeling it is all going down quite well. The spoken word sections of the show are met with increasing amounts of laughter in the right places. At one point I hear a sound like mute sobbing and realise it is actually someone laughing and trying to stop themselves. This is great as it makes other people laugh too, so it spreads around the pub. At the same time I hear a rising tide of noise from the corner, where a group of lads have got bored and started talking, raising their voices to compete with the PA. Also, drinkers have been pouring into the public bar, so the level of background noise is ramping up all the time and, missing the amplifiers in the sound desk, I cannot compete. Despite all of this, I keep going and the songs come out pretty much as they should. The final number is my campaign song, 'On the Road Not Taken', and loads of people clap along, so I get the Frank Turner feeling of having built a community, here in the Old Town Inn. Then I mistime the entry into the chorus so everyone is suddenly clapping on the offbeat, which causes confusion and most people stop. I notice the lady from the folk club adjusting her clapping to the correct beat and carrying on throughout.

Then it is all over and I feel nothing but relief. I am not being paid for this gig and have to be reminded to pass a hat around, sending a blue trilby, borrowed from Carnwethers, on a journey around the bar. I stay by the stage and am approached by a stream of audience members who have enjoyed the show, including the lady from the folk club, who says nothing about me appropriating the PA. When the hat comes back there is £178.12 in there, much more than I have earned from any gig so far. Paul adds to it with another £20 from the till and pours me a pint of Cornish lager that I carry in the car to Carnwethers, where Louise raids the fridge to make a ham and salad wrap.

The boat returns to Penzance late on Monday afternoon, where I spend the night, as I have a photoshoot in Cornwall the next morning. I stay in the cheapest Airbnb I can find. As soon as I arrive, having dragged my bags all the way from the harbour, the landlord leads me to a pile of dusty old books about music and asks me for a valuation, as he can see I am a musician. When I say I can't help, he offers another pile of books for free, which I decline as I have so much stuff in my bag I can barely move as it is. After that he disappears and I never see him again. There is, however, always a suspicion of weed in the air. I make a cup of tea in a kitchen that reminds me of my own: slices of white bread fan out of a loaf, the sink is full of dirty dishes and a half-used pack of butter lies open on the worktop, melting and coated with toast crumbs.

The next day I meet Jay in the car park by the station and we drive to a country lane leading to the sea near St Just. A former student of mine with a magnificent ability to make things happen, Jay organised the stage at Porthleven and is also launching *Elementum*, a magazine to showcase new writing alongside her prodigious photography. I am writing a piece about my travels and the pictures will illustrate the story. Walking down the misty lane, with the sea in the background and me looking thoughtful and poised after a gig on Saturday night, this photoshoot seems like a glimpse into the temple of rock stardom. I tell Jay the story of my paranoia on stage and she responds with two statements that are so obvious I really should have thought of them myself. Straight away I write them down so I will never forget.

- Always eat before a gig
- You can't tell what an audience is thinking by looking at their faces.

Clean Up Woman, 1977

Back at home the electric guitar is brought out for visitors as if it were a souvenir from a distant universe. Adults often think an electric guitar is plugged straight into the mains like a Hoover, so I have to explain the principles of amplification to bemused guests. We have a cleaner now called Gladys – though Mum insists I call her a home-help – and when she comes for her weekly dusting and hoovering session, I demonstrate the guitar, running through the different sounds I make. She chooses a favourite, the mellowest of them all, and Mum agrees. Then I turn up the volume to make an angry buzzsaw noise and play a few distorted chords that are so loud they both stagger backwards to the door, repeating the old refrain of how our entire generation will be deaf by the time we are forty. I tell them I don't really see the point of worrying about my hearing or being forty, because the bomb will blow us to oblivion anyway. Angry, distorted chords are wrung from the guitar until they are both safely out of the room and downstairs.

To try and stop me becoming a self-centred teenager,

I am given household chores. To begin with I clean shoes and take black plastic sheets – designed to stop Tigger, our long-haired cat leaving fur clumps on fabric – off the sofa and armchairs every morning. Now, alongside Dad, I do the drying-up as well, but can get out of this if I claim urgent homework. The subject that works best is history, as I can always say another chapter from another history book must be read by tomorrow. What I actually do is pick up the electric guitar and play it unplugged, which works well as Mum and Dad have the radio on downstairs. One night Mum gets suspicious and creeps after me. Because I am too busy posing with the guitar I do not hear the creaking stairs and when Mum bursts into the room to find me with the guitar in my hands, I feel my whole secret world has been laid bare for her to see.

Working on the Highway, 2016

It is a warm afternoon in April and I am sitting in Sarah Moody's little studio in Bristol with the door open, a guitar on my lap and tea and biscuits by my side. The next gig feels like the big one as people are paying proper money to come and see me, so I thought it a good idea to ask a proper musician to join me on stage. We are spending the afternoon adding cello parts to the songs. The gig is at the Egg Theatre in Bath and is significant as most of my theatre shows have started life here, loads of people I know are coming and I do not want to cock it up. The show also represents a step up as I am playing two fifty-minute sets, there is no support act and it has been advertised in the theatre brochure. Sarah agreed to take part ages ago, but is extremely busy juggling multiple bands, sessions, theatre shows and voluntary work, so by the time I get around to fixing up rehearsal times, there are only two dates left before the show. When we have finished this afternoon, she is driving to Calais to volunteer in a kitchen at the Jungle refugee camp for a week, giving us just one more rehearsal the day before the show itself. There is nothing to do but put paranoia and nervousness aside and concentrate on the music. We work hard and it is lovely to hear the songs come to life once again as Sarah surprises with each musical arrangement. The show is a week away, which is far enough for the rehearsal to be all pleasure. At the end of the afternoon I ride home on the train with the guitar propped against my legs, feeling I have done a decent day's work as a musician, which is something that never happens when I play on my own in the kitchen.

The Jack, 1978

We are tired of youth clubs and their middle-aged leaders telling us to turn down the sound. We want to be part of something like the gigs we see in Folkestone on a Saturday night. So, inspired by the punks who have torn up the rule book, we do it all ourselves. We hire the Cinque Ports Pavilion on Hythe seafront and design the posters, get the tickets printed, and book Barry and his disco. Our mums and dads agree to be bouncers. Once the gig is booked we learn more songs, so back in the Whitegates day room I growl my way through a catchy number about venereal disease that is popular at school. 'The Jack', by AC/DC, is easy to play and has a chorus that the boys join in. Then we learn 'All Right Now' by Free. As we practise one evening I play a solo. It is not the one on the record but just comes into my head and I discover I can carry on while Paul and Andy keep the rhythm going underneath. I glance at my reflection in the window and adjust my posture to look as cool as possible, then drop down onto my knees and lean right back with my eyes shut.

I wake up nervous on the morning of the show. In my fantasy life as a rock star I had not imagined anxiety could darken an otherwise sunny day. It is Saturday so I go to work at the jeweller's shop from nine to five-thirty. Sometimes, while serving a customer, I forget what is coming and the sun comes out, but then I remember and the sky darkens again. I can't say what is making me anxious, but know that the moment of standing in front of the microphone fills me with dread as well as excitement. After work I head back to Hythe, change out of my suit and help the others load our equipment in the back of Dad's car.

The Cinque Ports Pavilion was built on the promenade in the 1960s and has big windows looking directly out to sea. It is getting dark as we pull the curtains and set up our amplifiers on a makeshift stage made from wooden boxes. There is so much to do I forget I am nervous. Once again we have arranged to borrow Barry's disco speakers for my vocals and these are already set up by his record decks. I ask Barry if the speakers can be repositioned either side of the stage and, very politely, he refuses. I am annoyed but remain calm.

'If the speakers are to one side,' I say, 'then it'll seem as if my vocals aren't part of what's happening on stage.' Barry shakes his head, unmoved. 'It won't be *professional*,' I say, sounding a bit annoyed now. To look *professional* is the thing I want more than anything else. Once again Barry refuses, explaining he likes the speakers positioned near to his decks and that is an end to it. My voice gets higher as I lose my temper. 'People are coming to see *us*, not you,' I scream at him. 'How dare you fuck it up.' Barry looks impassive and coils a cable around his arm. 'We're paying you. Remember that,' I say, before spinning around and marching away. The disco speakers remain where they are on either side of the record decks.

Pilot of the Airwaves, 2016

I get a call from the theatre to say not enough tickets have been sold. I know people will turn up and pay on the door, but need to generate more advance publicity, so I get in touch with someone I know on **BBC Radio Bristol** and am invited to appear on the Saturday morning programme to chat and play a song live on air. I started working on live radio in 1986 and in the last thirty years have produced, directed and spoken on thousands of programmes, but never, ever come anywhere near to singing live on air. At Radio Scilly the interview was recorded and when it came to the bit where I had to play the songs I had several false starts before we recorded a usable take. This time there would be no retakes. So now, on top of the tension created by the show, there is a new anxiety at singing live on the radio. When I had a job here at the BBC, my office overlooked the path where guitar-wielding singer-songwriters would pass on their way between reception and the Radio Bristol studios. I used to be jealous of how relaxed they seemed as they sauntered towards their live sessions. Now, as I sit in reception making jokes with the security guards, I realise how easy it is to appear outwardly relaxed while an inner voice is screaming, 'Stop this now.' That voice is ignored as the producer leads me across the car park and into the cubicle outside the studio. As he makes me a cup of tea I tune up and practise the picking pattern of the song and as I do the presenter of another show walks by and stops to listen, closing his eyes and saying, 'Ah, that's lovely,' before moving on again. Such small moments of generous affirmation are riches to the nervous musician.

I am taken into the studio to meet the presenter, Laura Rawlings, already on air. I am to be interviewed alongside a graffiti artist and Laura puts us both at ease with genuine interest in our stories. The talking part is easy, as I thought it would be; the real challenge comes with the music. I have decided to sing 'Poppysong' as that is the best received song at my gigs. Laura asks me to introduce it then gives me the cue to start playing. My fingers do the job reasonably well, but as I play the introduction I am aware of the movement of each one and how thin the sound seems to be. I think of the strangeness of being in this airless room and my song playing out on radios in cars and houses around the city. For most people I will be part of the background, but I wonder if anyone has turned their radio up to listen, making a note of my name and look for the song on the internet, which is what I do all the time. Laura is busy setting up the next segment of the show, so the only person who is definitely listening is my fellow guest, the street artist. Despite 'Poppysong' being part of my repertoire for months, I am terrified of forgetting the words on air, so have printed them out and have them in front of me, which is oddly distracting. As I begin the second verse, I see a friend appear on the other side of the studio window. She smiles, starts to wave then realises I am actually live and stops her hand mid-air. At the end of the song both Laura and the artist applaud and I breathe again. My son Fred was listening and said the song was good but he could tell I was nervous.

All Right Now, 1979

We have managed to sell over a hundred tickets for the Cinque Ports Pavilion and a river of teens arrive all at once amid clouds of Babe perfume, Blue Stratos and Brut 33 aftershave. Our parents are stationed on the door with a bottle of wine and Andy's Alsatian dog. They check tickets and try to stop alcohol being brought into the hall. Some of the girls conceal spirits in their handbags, but the boys stash beer cans in the flower beds outside and keep coming in and going out for a drink. At one point Dad sends home a boy so drunk he walks over the top of cars parked outside.

By half past eight the dance floor is packed. I have decided we will come on at nine, and as our performance time approaches we take guitars and drumsticks downstairs, so we can make an entrance by coming back up again. Despite our argument earlier in the evening, Barry announces the band with enthusiasm. 'It's time for the main event. Let's hear it for the Entangled Network!' he shouts, like the ringleader of a circus. From downstairs, we hear this and the cheer that follows. Recently at the cinema I saw the Led Zeppelin film

The Song Remains the Same, and want to recreate the bit where the band process through a network of subterranean tunnels on their way to the stage. There are no tunnels here, so we make do by marching around the lower level of the Cinque Ports Pavilion and up the single flight of stairs. I had hoped everyone in the hall would pack themselves around the stage and while a few have, most have headed for the sides and wonder what to do next. The cheers have subsided by the time we reach the top of the stairs, so we walk across the dance floor and onto the stage in silence.

We do not hang about and kick things off with 'Johnny B. Goode'. A couple of friends at the front nod their heads and some who had scuttled to the sides come creeping forward again. When we play 'The Jack' the boys all join in – the girls, I notice, look disgusted – and when we get to the opening chords of 'All Right Now' our friend Chris shakes his head as if he is properly freaking out. Although I am too inhibited to dance at a disco, I'm quite happy jigging about on stage in front of a hundred people, dropping to my knees and contorting my face when I play a solo, and jumping in the air when I play the final chord of a song. Every so often Dad comes up the stairs and I see his face break into a smile as he looks over the crowd to the stage. 'Hello, Hythe, how you doin'?' I say, mimicking the stage patter of the touring bands I have seen in Folkestone. When there is only a muted response, I repeat the words again, shouting into the microphone. 'I SAID, HELLO, HYTHE, HOW YOU DOIN'?'

See You at the Show, 2016

After my appearance on the radio, the only thing to do with the rest of the weekend is to practise, which I do in the kitchen, running songs over and over again. Until I saw Frank Turner, I played sitting down, but ever since I've been standing up to perform. Apart from the odd leap into the air at the end of a song, I feel a bit awkward standing at the microphone. While on stage at the Old Town Inn, I took my guitar off for the spoken sections and managed to get the strap caught around my legs. I had to untangle myself three times during the gig. So I decide for this next show I will sit down. Rehearsing with Sarah Moody on Monday, I push my voice to compete with the cello, and travelling home again realise I have strained my vocal cords. I sip honey-and-ginger tea and try not to talk.

On the day of the show I wake feeling strangely calm. I go for a long run and while out, remember an incident the day before my finals at Winchester. The exams began with a paper about playwright Bertolt Brecht. It was late afternoon when I walked to the water meadows to sit quietly and begin revision. Under my arm was a folder of notes unread since the lectures. I had not done a stroke of work. A friend from the course came past on a bicycle and I asked if he was taking a break. He told me he had finished revising as there was nothing we could do now, what with the exam being tomorrow. I had not even started and the encounter made me feel sick. That has pretty much been the story of my whole life. Now, running across Bristol Downs on a fine spring morning, I am ready for what is to come.

I head to Bath at lunchtime. The day is bright and warm and I enjoy the sun on my skin as I walk through the city towards the theatre. I am early and am given the keys to dressing room two on the top floor. I make a herbal tea and look through a little window over the rooftops of Bath. When our technician arrives we spend an hour sorting out mics, stands and lights before Sarah turns up. All the time I feel prepared and locked into the task ahead. Sarah and I rehearse in the empty theatre as the sound is adjusted around us. At six we stop and break. I step outside but the bright sunny world is too much, so I head for the dressing room, where I heat up a stew with rice in a recycled takeaway container. I learned from my experience at the Old Town Inn and the meal helps to calm me, though when I try to sing I feel my voice on the edge of damage.

Sarah offers to lead a vocal warm-up, which helps both voice and focus. We blow and we puff and make strange siren-like noises. It is seven o'clock now and showtime is galloping towards us. In the dressing room I put on the polka dot shirt I reserve for gigs. We come down via a clinically white internal staircase and wait behind the curtain, where I hear my pre-show playlist of upbeat folk music playing over the buzz of talk and laughter. Then the music fades and the house lights go down, the talking stops, the stage lights go up and we walk out. I see nothing beyond the front row but hear a wave of applause from the darkness. There are plenty of people out there.

We start with 'Pelistry' and I lock into the rhythms of Sarah's cello. We sound good and the applause is big at the end. Performing this show is like riding a wave: I don't feel totally in control, I don't know if I'll remember the words, I don't know what my hands are supposed to do, but somehow the next thing keeps happening and words and music come out. I have a strange feeling about the Ewan MacColl song 'Shoals of Herring', so secrete the lyrics near my feet, hidden by the stage monitor. Although I can't see who is out in the audience, I am able to have fun and detect a real sense of sadness when I reach the last part of the spoken story. 'On the Road Not Taken' is the final number and then it's all over and we stand behind the curtain on the edge of the stage listening to applause, cheering and stamping on the floor for an encore. My strained voice has held out for the whole show and everything has come together at last. On the way out of the building, Kate Cross – artistic director of the theatre and mentor and critic of my theatre work – offers a single suggestion. 'End the show with "Puff, the Magic Dragon",' she says. 'That's my only note.'

More, More, More, 1977

Before the gig my friends are primed to demand an encore and I tell Barry not to cut them off with a record. After the last chord we leave the stage and go halfway down the stairs to wait. Someone starts a steady clap, others join in, then people start stamping their feet and we hear a chorus of 'More, more, more', just like at the Leas Cliff Hall. I am enjoying hearing it so much, Andy has to push me back up the stairs. We run through the crowd like conquering heroes and play a frenzied version of 'Wild Thing'. At the end I wipe the sweat from my face with my shirtsleeves.

Taking off the guitar, I look across the Cinque Ports Pavilion as if it were a stadium packed full and hear the cheers of the crowd following us through the corridors to the limo that drives us to our waiting plane. What actually happens is Mum and Dad give me a lift home in their Austin Princess.

I had delegated the collection of door money to a friend and am handed a jam jar full of notes and coins. We count it on the floor and after taking off the cost of the hall have earned £125, which seems an absurdly large amount of money to make from something we enjoy so much. When Mum tells me it isn't a good idea to keep all that money under the bed, we open a joint bank account and use it to buy PA speakers of our own, as Andy thinks it unlikely that Barry will lend us his again.

Kitchen Man, 2016

The next morning I wake at six with my throat feeling as if I have been swallowing razor blades. I go downstairs to tackle a mountain of washing-up and the waste pipe beneath the sink breaks and floods the kitchen floor. Later in the day the boiler stops working. After all the excitement of last night it seems as though the universe is righting itself.

Cars, 1977

Sunday morning. The day after the gig at the Cinque Ports Pavilion. In the few steps it takes to get from the kitchen to the garage I hear a chorus of lawnmowers from the neighbouring gardens and smell fresh cut grass in the air. I am up much earlier than I would like and slightly resentful because musicians shouldn't get up until the afternoon. 'Nice of you to join me at last,' says Dad, who is wearing overalls and has oily hands. He wants to show me how to de-coke the engine of the Traveller. The car is in the garage and already the bonnet is up and the dark innards are waiting for spanners. The whole place stinks of petrol. 'We have to do this every 10,000 miles,' he says in a voice that irritates me straight away. I start to play a guitar solo in my head. 'Or less if the car is being used for shorter journeys.' The Morris is now our second car, used mainly by Mum, but it is Dad's pride and joy and he keeps it in pristine condition. Because I am about to learn to drive, Dad thinks it only fair that I should take part in the maintenance regime. I am hoping music will make so much money I can get someone to do the repairs for me. Dad has eliminated the tiniest spots of rust, replaced the rotting woodwork and lovingly coated the new wood with thick layers of translucent varnish. 'The first thing we're going to do is to release the head bolts,' says Dad. The Traveller is a car you can take apart, lay out greased on old towels, put back together again and have no bits left over; there are no complicated electronics to spoil the simple joy of mechanical engineering. But I have no interest in how it works, I just want to drive it so we can get to gigs on our own. 'Now the reason we do this is because of a build-up of carbon in the combustion chambers.'

As Dad explains what is clogging the arteries in the heart of the motor, I drift away from the guts of the machine, the little town of Hythe and the arc of the bay. I am on a road that takes me far away from here, to gig after gig, crowd after crowd and encore after encore. Dad becomes absorbed by the rhythm of his work and forgets to tell me what he is doing. I slip away unnoticed, back to my bedroom and the electric guitar not plugged in, to relive last night in silence.

Brislington Diamonds, 2016

Maybe I am getting used to it or maybe it is because there is only one song to sing, but this time there are no nerves. I run through 'Brislington Diamonds' once in the kitchen then head for Bristol Old Vic theatre, where I am playing in another 250th birthday show. It is Bank Holiday Monday and the streets are teeming with people in holiday mood. The road outside the theatre has been closed to traffic and seems like a festival, with food stalls and entertainment. I check in and go to a room in the loft to rehearse, but a trumpeter is already there and louder than me, so I go onto a walkway and run through the song a couple of times, singing to the rooftops of Bristol. Then I am taken backstage. The folk band are back again and use up most of the soundcheck time, so when I go on stage for my turn and do not have the right box to connect to the theatre sound system, a technician shoves a microphone in front of the guitar and tells me it will have to do. Back in the wings I meet a fellow performer and we muck about together, something unthinkable last time I was here. It almost feels normal to walk out onto the stage and look into the darkness, where 500 people are waiting. Remembering how Frank Turner galvanises his audience with rousing speeches between songs, and not knowing when I will get to play in front of 500 people again, I try out some Turner tactics: I make a passionate speech in celebration of the Old Vic that gets a loud cheer then launch straight into 'Brislington Diamonds', which passes in a moment. I want to keep moving back and forth off the microphone but can't, because if I do, the guitar drops out completely, so stay rooted to the spot. There is a big round of applause at the end and I stop on my way off to bow once more. Off stage I get a surreptitious thumbs-up from a fellow performer, but most people are too engrossed in their own preparations to notice my triumphant walk through the wings.

Afterwards, a couple of audience members stop me in the foyer to say they like the song, and when I look on YouTube the next day, there have been a few more views of the video. Suddenly, I am hit by the scale of what I am doing. I play to 500 random strangers and a few like what they hear enough to look me up. But to be honest, very few. How many times would I need to do this to have people want to come and see me? I remember our childhood blueprint for success, the secret hope that a single appearance on *Top of the Pops* would propel us into the rock stratosphere for ever. How far that is from the truth.

Thunder in the Night, 1978

As the months pass it becomes part of the routine, the three of us wheeling the equipment to the day centre at Whitegates to rehearse, then going off to play wherever we can, never far from Hythe. In the summer, we perform at a party on a farm in the country. We set up our equipment in the barn and leave the doors open when we soundcheck. I now own a distortion pedal that makes the guitar sound fuzzy and exciting, irrespective of what I play, and we run through a few songs as loud as we dare, riffing at cattle, who stare back with big, bemused eyes. Later a friend tells me she was being driven to the party when her parents stopped on a hilltop to look at the sunset. As they gazed over miles of misty countryside, they could hear the sound of the Entangled Network rolling across the fields of Kent like thunder.

On the Road Not Taken, 2016

I have been writing radio drama for the last twenty years and am commissioned by BBC Radio 4 to turn the story of my childhood musical experiences into a play. It is this radio version of *On the Road Not Taken* that has subsidised all my musical adventures so far this year. I mine the past to create dramatised scenes played by a cast of young actors, including a young version of me, and spend an afternoon recreating the sound of the Entangled Network in my living room at home. The play is framed by a description of walking on stage at the Bristol Old Vic and singing again after a three-decade hiatus. Now my school friend Fred and I are reunited, I ask him if he will join me to record 'On the Road Not Taken', the final song in the play. As he lives a few miles from the studio in Brighton everything falls into place. When I arrive, Fred is sitting in the kitchen of Pier Productions, cup of coffee in hand, long legs stretched out and mandolin case at his side. We walk up the stairs to the recording studio and have a few minutes to practise as microphones are set up. I sent Fred a simple recording of the song from my phone from which he has written a mandolin part. As soon as we play it is like being back in the day room at Whitegates. The same musicality that drew me to Fred at secondary school is all there and his mandolin weaves a detailed accompaniment to my strumming. I think of my boyhood self, watching Fred leave the Whitegates day room, in 1977, believing the dream was over. Now here we are, reunited nearly forty years later, and the first thing we do is make a recording to be transmitted on national radio. It could be a wonderful ending or a whole new beginning.

Heartbreak Hotel, 1979

Andy and I decide to broaden our horizons and set off on the bus to Folkestone looking for a gig. In a Victorian square in the West End of town is the Springfield Hotel. They call their basement bar the Folkestone Jazz Centre and have live music a few nights a week. I sense an opportunity. We march in without an appointment and demand to see the manager. A harassed man appears and carefully listens to my lyrical description of the Entangled Network, not in any way a jazz band, I admit, but an ensemble that would be honoured to play in his venue. 'We might,' I suggest, 'open the Folkestone Jazz Centre to a whole new audience who'll come back for the actual jazz.' When he tells us it is hard to pull a jazz crowd on a Saturday night, I tell him our band would have no trouble making the place buzz. The manager looks sceptical but agrees to give us a try, on the condition we are not paid. We say yes and are taken down to the basement where the walls are painted dark blue, there are low ceilings and a lingering smell of damp is in the air. Andy and I both look around, nodding vigorously. There is no stage, the manager explains, because the ceiling is too low; we will play in the bay window. We shake hands and set a date in a month's time. At long last, Folkestone is in our sights.

I Wanna Be Your Dog, 2016

I am booked to play at a theatre in a converted shop in Clevedon, North Somerset. As Sarah Moody is busy playing her cello at a festival, I will perform the show on my own. Stage fright no longer dominates; I sleep well the night before and am still calm as I walk down the access road of a modern shopping centre and into the back of Theatre Shop. Sitting on stage to soundcheck it is disconcerting to look out of the windows to a precinct full of Saturday shoppers. With an hour and a half to go I wander over the road to a pub and order food. When it doesn't come after ten minutes I start to feel tense and realise I am nervous now.

Back at the theatre I sit alone in the little dressing room on the first floor, looking down at shuttered shopfronts and the occasional teenager speeding through the precinct on a skateboard. There is a kettle, some teabags, a mirror and a clothes rail on which are hanging costumes from another show. The bar is outside my dressing room, so I hear the conversation and laughter building as the audience arrives. It peaks then fades when they go downstairs to take their seats. I am learning how lonely it can be for a performer out on their own. I am the reason the audience are here but cannot join in with their conversations and laughter. I would quite like to be enjoying Saturday night too, having a drink and watching someone play, rather than cranking myself up to perform for the next hour and a half. And there it is: performing a show is not a more intense version of watching a show, it is something else entirely, like the difference between reading a book and writing one. I am at work. It might be a great job and one that lots of people would like to do, but it is a job and like all jobs it carries a responsibility. Then, there is a knock on the dressing-room door and the theatre technician gives me a two-minute call. I stand up and stare in the mirror to see my hair looking as if I have grown the ears of a King Charles Spaniel.

There are friends in the audience and the show goes well. I make mistakes but carry on, remembering the words of the great trumpeter, bandleader and composer Miles Davis, who said, 'It's not the note you play that's the wrong note – it's the note you play afterwards that makes it right or wrong.' At the end of the show I walk towards the curtain and am called back for an encore. I do what had been suggested in Bath and play 'Puff, the Magic Dragon', inviting the audience to join in with the chorus. Everybody does and from the cheers that follow they seem to enjoy it too. I learn another important lesson: there is nothing that creates unity in an audience like singing together. When performer and audience sing as one, the barrier between them is broken down and the show becomes a participative event. When that happens, for a little while, the pressure is taken off me. I should have known this before – Frank Turner's gigs are one big singalong – but like so much of my journey, I need to discover these things myself.

Beg, Steal or Borrow, 1979

Mum and Dad do not understand why those of us in bands lend and borrow equipment as much as we do. The truth is, nobody has all the gear they need, so we loan stuff to each other. It is a sort of favour bank. But Mum and Dad think Fred is taking advantage of me, because his parents call at the house regularly to borrow an amplifier I bought from him a few months back. They tell a story with consequences stretching into the future, where I lend so much stuff I am barely left with the clothes I am standing in. One Sunday morning, when I am tired and hungover, Fred's mum and dad come to get the amplifier again and I, out of nowhere, deliver a speech that voices everything my parents have been saying to me. 'It is really time this lending stopped,' I say. 'This amplifier belongs to me now and Fred should buy his own. It's ridiculous, borrowing his own amplifier back again, week after week. Enough is enough.' Fred's mum and dad look shocked, but say nothing and drive off with the amplifier in the back of the car. The trouble is, I have on long-term loan Fred's sustain pedal, which is a little box that sits at my feet at gigs. When I press a footswitch, the guitar becomes a shrieking noise that makes a simple riff sound really good. Afterwards, Fred keeps his cool, saying nothing at school, although he is slightly more distant and stops offering helpful advice.

Coal Not Dole, 2016

Two days later I travel to the Cotswolds to lead a session at a storytelling conference in a Gothic mansion overlooking the Stroud valley. In the evening there is a concert and participants are invited to perform. I have travelled by train and am cycling the last part of the journey, so cannot carry a guitar. I bring the shruti box instead, but even that makes my backpack feel heavy as I pedal up the steep hill out of Stroud town. I have not been in the countryside for weeks and summer has exploded: trees hang heavy with leaves, tall grass and wildflowers line the roadside verges and the hedgerows are alive with blackbird song.

Tonight is important as it is exactly the sort of event I have sat through for the last thirty years wishing I had the confidence to perform. After dinner everyone assembles in the main hall. The compère explains that only he knows the running order so there is no point in any of us being nervous. I am the third on, walk to the front and breathe deeply in and out before saying anything. The audience are formed into a large semicircle with big windows behind so I look out across the valley to a vast cumulous cloudscape in the sky above the Cotswolds. I sing 'Coal Not Dole' and preface the song with the story of travelling across Kent in the back of our Morris Traveller to see my grandmother and passing through the middle of the mining village of Snowdown. I was excited by the sight of the pithead gear and the possibility of a steam train in the sidings, where they carried on working after being abolished from the main lines of England. I tell how we were once taken on a primary school trip down Snowdown mine, rode through dark tunnels alongside black-faced miners and crawled up to the coalface. Then I describe the song being written when the pit was threatened with closure, by a woman called Kay Sutcliffe, who lives in the village, and how, via the singing of Oysterband, the story made its way into the world. Then I shut my eyes to sing and it comes out easily. Afterwards two women come and talk to me. I can see they have been crying. They tell me they live in a valley town in South Wales, decimated by the mine closure in the 1980s, and the song has told their story.

This, this is what a song can do.

Could It Be Magic, 1979

It is the night of our first gig at the Springfield Hotel. I get home from work, change into clean jeans, white T-shirt and pinstripe jacket and head for Whitegates, where our transport has arrived. We have two friends who have passed their driving tests and are keen to show off, so they stand waiting in front of a beige Austin Maxi and a rusting Ford Escort, swinging car keys around their fingers. Our mums and dads are not needed any more. I sit low in the back seat of the Escort as we drive along the seafront, looking at the blue channel, excited to be on the road at last, even if the road is only leading to Folkestone, which is five miles away. As we carry our equipment down to the basement bar, we pass a poster for the gig. Over the date somebody has written TONITE with a fat black felt-tip pen.

When we start to play, the bar is full of friends, who all get served despite most being underage. Some are sitting at small tables and others stand in the gaps so the place feels full and buzzing. There are also loads of people I have never seen before, including two identical twin sisters who chain-smoke and stare without smiling. Fred is in the audience too and I know that he knows his sustain pedal is at my feet. He is as still as a statue, face impassive, not betraying any emotion and when I ask everyone to sing 'The Jack', Fred doesn't join in. Neither do the two sisters, but I see them whisper into each other's ears and look at me.

I have never heard of magic mushrooms. So when a wizened guy comes up between songs, sticks a coin bag full of miniature fungi under my nose and tells me to help myself, I think it is a joke. I have one, another, then another and so it goes on. Nothing happens. The more we play, the more our audience have to drink, the louder they get and the more fun we all have. Halfway through the set I glance at Andy, sweating in his check shirt as he thrashes the drums and Paul's head dancing as he powers through basslines, and I think I love them, love this band and what we are becoming. We are still raw and unformed, but have made all this happen tonight and it is nothing to do with school, teachers or parents. On a bookshelf at home I have an anthology of writing from *Rolling Stone* magazine. There is a picture of Keith Richards, shirtless, standing on a rock, looking over an immense canyon. The picture is subtitled, 'Your rules don't apply to me.' And that is how I feel tonight, in the Springfield Hotel. We encore, as we always do, with 'Wild Thing' and I press the footswitch on the sustain pedal so the guitar screams, then drop to my knees and jump up into the air.

Afterwards I lean my guitar against the back wall and head

to the bar, passing Fred who remains sitting still and doesn't catch my eye. I am intercepted by one of the twin sisters who has bought me a drink and carries it to her table, signalling for me to sit between them both. They are eighteen years old, German and living and working in Folkestone for a year to improve their English. They have their own flat. 'I think you will be my boyfriend,' says one of the sisters, kissing me on the lips while the other looks away. It feels more like a statement than a question. In all the gigs throughout the years in youth clubs, church halls, old people's homes and parties, my musical adventures have failed to lead to a single encounter with a girl. I think again of *Stardust*, and the scene with the naked women in the recording studio. Perhaps it is happening at last. Then the sisters speak to each other in German and the one who kissed me pulls out her diary. First she takes my phone number, then starts to count the weeks ahead, writing an entry in three months' time. 'This is when we will sleep together,' says my new girlfriend, showing me the date, then closing the diary with a finality implying negotiations are over. We are going to a party after the gig and I try to persuade the sisters to join us. 'No,' says my new girlfriend. 'We have to be somewhere else.' Then she kisses me again and they get up and leave. When I pack away my guitar I see the sustain pedal is missing. Apparently Fred unplugged it, dropped it into his pocket and walked into the night. Before we go, the mushroom man appears by my side and tells me to finish off the rest of the bag.

245

Leaving on a Jet Plane, 2016

The next gig is in Berlin but I wake up feeling so rough I consider pulling out. It is a week since the Brexit referendum and England feels strange and unfamiliar. A rift has opened up and Twitter and Facebook are full of accusations and arguments. And I seem to be coming down with a cold. Then I remember the trouble my friend Louisa has gone to, in order to make this happen: finding a venue, putting up posters, rounding up an audience. On top of this, four more friends are having a weekend in Berlin and have chosen this date because I am performing. So I have another honey-and-ginger tea and wonder how to repair my guitar case so it makes it to the other end. The man in the local hardware shop tells me the answer is Gorilla Tape and a big sign saying FRAGILE. I go from there to lose the spaniel ears and while in the chair my hairdresser asks if I have a busy weekend ahead. 'Got a gig in Berlin,' I say as casually as possible, as if it is the sort of thing that happens all the time. My hairdresser nods as if it is the sort of thing all his customers say and we leave it at that, but sitting in the chair I am really excited. I have a gig in Berlin at the weekend.

The internet is full of horror stories about guitars getting broken in transit. The most consistent advice is to make sure the instrument does not rattle around in its case, so I pack it in with socks and pants to restrict movement. At Berlin Schönefeld Airport I wait at the luggage carousel as everyone on my flight collects their luggage. I am left alone and there is no sign of the guitar. Then a man in uniform comes through a distant door and gently puts the guitar case down on the far side of the hall. It is like being reunited with an old friend.

I take the U-Bahn across the city to meet Louisa from work, then travel to her apartment in Wedding, a district in former East Berlin. There is chipped brown paintwork on the street door and some graffiti in blue spray-paint, above which is a picture of me smiling on a poster. Louisa lives in a block set around a central courtyard, which we walk through before heading up a staircase in an echoing hallway to the fifth floor. The apartment has a little shaded balcony looking over a smaller courtyard, which is like a secret in the middle of the city. A woman waves from a nearby window and Louisa says she will probably be in the audience tomorrow.

Next evening I head out of the apartment and down the road with my guitar case. All day I have been wandering around the neighbourhood, mercifully free of anxiety, and enjoying a heatwave in the city. The Ufer Café is on the ground floor of an apartment block opposite a canal. The entrance is an archway in a wall covered by foliage, so a beer sign above the pavement is the only clue to what is within.

We are in the middle of the Euro 2016 football tournament and a huge TV screen has been set up in the garden to show the games. Inside, I am welcomed by Falke, the owner of the bar, who is a large man with grey stubble and a deep voice. He gestures to the small stage and tells me to set up. At the bar, a couple are having an early evening drink, and they watch me carefully as I plug the guitar into the tuning pedal and run a cable into the PA, which is a single speaker on one side of the stage. I fiddle with the volume control and try a couple of songs. Both Falke and the customers listen and tell me I am sounding good. I start to relax and take in the surroundings. We are in a small room with round tables and a low ceiling. There are pictures of musicians all over the walls and a sign above the stage that reads *Not Older But Better.* The shelves behind the bar are lined with bottles of spirits and liqueurs and a clock made from a cymbal is fixed to the wall above. Even when completely empty, the Ufer Café feels like somewhere exotic; exactly the sort of place I hoped I would end up when all this began.

It takes me a while to realise everyone is smoking; here in Berlin you can still smoke in bars as long as food isn't being served. I am hoping the couple who heard the soundcheck have been impressed enough to stay, but in broken English they tell me they have a meal to cook at home and gather their things, wish me luck and leave. Falke offers a beer but I decline, setting up a water glass on the stage. I walk out to the street to feel the warm evening sun on my face and see, coming down the road, Louisa and my four friends from the UK. It is a wonderful thing to see familiar faces so far from home and we hug and take pictures of each other in the street. People start arriving at the bar, buying drinks and heading out to the garden, where the TV is showing the Wales versus Belgium game. When I start to play, the audience are mostly my friends, though others in the garden station themselves close to the door, so when the football crowd roars they rush out and watch the game. In the interval I go outside and get immersed in the second half of the match. Wales might win and the predominantly German audience is backing them, so I postpone the start of the second half until the game is over.

When the final whistle blows and Wales has beaten Belgium 3-1, the mood is euphoric. Everyone pours in from the garden and buys a drink and I go back onto the little stage. Since I arrived in Berlin, Germans have been asking me about the referendum, as though they cannot quite believe the result. I open the set with 'Let Union Be', an uptempo version of an old folk song I have learned from the folk big band Bellowhead. 'Let Union Be' takes on a new significance here in Berlin and is followed by a mighty cheer. Now safely into the second half, I decide to make the most of the free beer on offer and achieve exactly the right level of intoxication, where everything sounds and feels great. At the end we all sing 'Puff, the Magic Dragon' and I hear the chorus coming back in a German accent. There is a hat on the bar and when Falke passes it to me later it is packed full of euros.

During the show I tell my story about liking the band Mud – even out here in Germany it gets a laugh. In fact the story has been going down so well over recent gigs I have been playing it up a bit. Mud seems to be a byword for the naff end of the 1970s pop scene and their name never fails to amuse. I wondered whether the Germans would know who they are, but they do and they laugh. Afterwards, as Falke is pulling me another beer, he tells how he grew up in the old East Germany where there was no pop music. One day Mud came to play. They were the first live band he saw and that night he recognised the visceral power of rock and roll. Falke points around this bar, making sure I understand the connection between him seeing Mud and the path that led him to this place where I have just played. 'Every music must live,' he tells me.

Later, I am tapped on the shoulder by a friendly young guy with a guitar case on his shoulder. Aldo is a Brazilian bass player who had heard about my show but couldn't come, as he was playing another gig across town. When I say it is a shame we were not able to play together he says, 'We can, right now.' So we set up and start to jam, virtuoso bass lines weaving around my chords. Then we are joined by Petra, a singer from Spain, and launch into a rousing version of the old Mexican folk song turned rock and roll hit 'La Bamba'. The night ends with Falke singing, unaccompanied and unamplified, the Leonard Cohen song 'Hallelujah', his rich baritone silencing all conversation.

It is past four and the sky streaked with dawn as we leave the bar and head back to Louisa's apartment, still pleasantly drunk, guitar case in hand, feeling a tiny sense of what it must be like to be Dylan, Springsteen, Turner and all the other troubadours who have travelled this road before me.

Purple Haze, 1979

After our triumphant performance at the Springfield Hotel, we load up the cars and our drivers take us to the party. I can still taste mushrooms in my mouth. Along the seafront I open the window to feel the wind on my face, savouring the sensation of gig, girlfriend and party on the same night. I watch the sea, the horizon and the flashing of channel-marker buoys and lighthouses, but the more I look, the more everything seems to be melting together. Then we arrive at the party and I sit in a black leather office chair and am spun around. The whole room blurs until it feels I am spinning inside a solid shaft made of blurry party faces and wallpaper. 'You're tripping, man,' shouts somebody, who seems far away at the end of a very long tunnel.

I do not hear from the German girl for three days. Then one night, at a quarter past ten, the phone rings. Mum answers. There is a rule in the house that the phone is not to be used – incoming or outgoing – after nine at night unless it is a severe emergency. I hear Mum's voice, clipped and angry. 'Do you know what time it is? We were just going to bed. No you can't speak to him, please call back tomorrow.' The girl doesn't call for another three days and when we eventually speak – at half past seven in the evening – she says, 'I am not your girlfriend any more.'

But I don't care because I'm in a band and there will be plenty more girls and plenty more parties too.

Hendra, 2016

So far this year I have gone from singing two songs in public, through being a support act, to performing my own show and travelling abroad to play in a foreign city. Although the road will not end at the *Top of the Pops* studio, it feels like I have been heading in the right direction. The final gig of the season is at the festival I love the most, Port Eliot in Cornwall.

Soon after leaving my job as a producer at the BBC, I started teaching at Falmouth University and have made many friends in the county: generations of students, performers, lecturers and people I have met along the way. Once a year they all come together at this country estate on the banks of the River Tiddy, surrounded by rolling hills and farmland. I have had some of the best nights of my life here. To make it even more exciting I am to perform on the Caught By The River stage, where in the past I have stood and watched incredible musicians strutting their stuff in a marquee packed with appreciative revellers. To be completely honest, I hadn't actually been booked by the organisers; that offer had come from my friend, the author Tim Dee, who had a slot and suggested we share the stage and my songs be part of a sequence of readings. The main man behind this venue is Jeff Barrett, founder of the Heavenly Recordings record label, who numbers the Manic Street Preachers, Saint Etienne and Beth Orton among his signings. Although I harbour no illusions about being spotted and signed myself, there is something exciting about performing in the presence of someone with so much history. And a little bit of hope for… something.

Sarah and I arrive on Saturday afternoon when the festival is halfway through and wander around the site, pausing in the wellbeing field, walking by the river, eating greasy onion bhajis while listening to a talk from sometime guitarist of The Fall, Brix Smith. I realise that performing at a festival is very different to going to one, or at least it is before the performance has taken place. Although it is lovely being here, I can't let go and enjoy myself fully, because tomorrow I will be on stage. The anxiety is nothing like the darkness of earlier in the year, more a soft shadow cast over the future, but it stops me from properly being part of it all.

St German's Church on the Port Eliot estate is one of the concert venues at the festival. Here, early on Saturday evening, we watch a gig by Ben Watt and Bernard Butler. Ben Watt is a songwriter, DJ, producer and the other half of Everything But The Girl, and Bernard Butler is a virtuoso guitarist and former member of the band Suede. It is a lovely show as Ben's songs have walked me through the years and hearing them tonight takes me on a journey that loops back in time then returns to the present with 'Hendra', the title track of a recent album. All is going very well until the final verse when Ben forgets the words. What he does next is a lesson in performance, as he keeps playing while admitting what has happened and asks if anyone can help. Lots of people know the song and call out the words, but Ben can't hear over the noise of the PA, so a woman looks up the lyrics on her phone, then goes up to the stage and holds it in front of his face. Far from seeming like a mistake, this whole episode becomes a story that we all want to end well, so when it does and the song finishes we jump to our feet, applauding. In the world of recorded sound, near perfection is usually the objective, but here, at a gig, not everything goes according to plan. Which is like life really. Mistakes happen, so when they do, make them part of the show.

Because of the gig tomorrow, Sarah and I pass up the chance to dance all night at a disco in the woods and retire to our little tent at half past ten. I soften wax earplugs with my fingers until they are malleable enough to be jammed into my ears to mute the sound of the main stage down the hill, broadcasting a four-to-the-floor bass beat that carries on until dawn.

Because we are among the first to sleep we are also the first up and enjoy the stillness of a sunny morning, eating breakfast in the open air, sitting on a wall by the main house watching the festival come alive. By Sunday afternoon there is a sense of weariness in the air. As I carry the guitar towards my stage, I meet a man called Parker, who has been resident DJ at the Caught By The River stage all weekend. He is squinting in the bright afternoon sunshine, looking sunbaked and exhausted. 'I'm knackered,' he tells me. 'I've been on it since Thursday. I'm heading for a kip.'

When I soundcheck on stage, my voice and guitar sound better in the monitors than ever before. On either side is the big PA system that has pumped music into the crowd all weekend. This feels like the real thing. Then, Tim and I are announced and walk on to the stage to look at a crowd of about thirty people, sitting on benches scattered around a marquee that can fit several hundred. It is half past three in the afternoon and broad daylight, so I can see the expression on everybody's face and most people look shattered. Because I am on my favourite stage at my favourite festival, I have decided to go the full Frank Turner and am poised with my biggest, noisiest songs. In fact it was at Port Eliot in 2011 that I first saw Frank Turner play to a packed tent on a Saturday afternoon. The front third of the crowd knew all the words to all the songs and jumped up and down singing along, so everyone else was swept up by the infectious enthusiasm of it all. Somewhere beneath conscious thought I hope that will happen this afternoon, choosing to ignore the fact that at this time on Sunday, the audience want a rest from raucousness and prefer something muted and quiet. I kick off with 'Brislington Diamonds' and right away feel the power of the PA system. The guitar is punchy, cutting above the ambient noise that drifts into the tent from nearby sound systems. When I start to sing my voice feels full, rich, rounded and powerful; I don't have to give too much to make a big noise and I work the microphone, getting close for quieter moments, then pulling back and letting rip in the chorus, finding at last a raspy, rock vocal sound. Everything in the last three years has led to this moment and it feels good. After the first chorus there is a little guitar riff and I take this moment to look around the tent. Most of the thirty or so audience members are sitting completely still with no discernible expression on their faces. Then I spot Jeff Barrett on a wooden bench, halfway down the left-hand side of the tent, slumped slightly forward. As I play I watch his head sink into his hands, where it stays. When I look again he has disappeared completely.

And with that I am off the road for the rest of the year.

Afterglow, 1980

The Entangled Network go on to have an illustrious career. We organise more parties, become regulars at the Springfield Hotel and even travel in the back of a van to far-off Dover – which is thirteen miles away – to play to three men and a dog. When Paul leaves to concentrate on his CSEs we find someone else and carry on. We start mixing with bands who seem poised on the brink of something bigger and it feels as though we are carried by the same tide. Then one day in 1980 we go into Europa Sound Studios, which is in the basement of a terraced house in Folkestone, and make a demo tape. There is a frisson of excitement as the last person to record here was guitarist Henry McCullough, who had been in Wings with Paul McCartney and performed at Woodstock with Joe Cocker's band. The studio engineer coaxes a performance out of us, recording a backing track first, then adding a layer of guitar before putting the vocals on top, gluing the sounds together with subtle touches of echo and reverb. Hearing ourselves through the big studio speakers is so incredible I ask the engineer if he will do our sound on *Top of the Pops*. He sighs wearily, like he has heard all this before. 'That's a long and hard road, lads,' is all he says. Next day, when we listen to a cassette of the songs we realise that at last we really do sound like a proper band.

But my A levels are approaching and my predicted grades are so bad that Mum and Dad sit me down at the kitchen table for a talk.

'You're going to have to work really hard to pull this off,' says Dad. I try to tell them how much the band means to me and all the plans we have for the future.

'We just want you to have a choice,' says Mum. I know I am losing the argument so agree to put the band on hold. As soon as I do, Andy brings in someone else and I am out for good.

Then I mess up my exams anyway. So my Saturday job in a jeweller's shop in Folkestone becomes full time and I study in the evenings for retakes.

It is a dark evening in November 1981 when I walk from the shop to the Leas Cliff Hall to see a gig by the singer-songwriter Ralph McTell. All I know about him is a hit from the 1970s called 'Streets of London' that became the acceptable face of pop music, the sort of thing my parents like and is sung in the local Methodist church when they are being modern. But a friend has told me I should give this man a chance and I have taken his advice.

What follows that evening is a revelation. Alone with his guitar on a big stage, Ralph McTell sings songs, tells stories and sings songs that are stories. I realise that in all the years I have been making a racket I have forgotten the lesson learned when I heard 'Puff, the Magic Dragon'. I have forgotten how a simple song can change the shape of a day.

When I walk away at the end of the show I know there is nothing I want more than to go out on the road with a headful of songs and stories.

But that is not what happens. I do try it once, in a café called the Monk's Kitchen in Folkestone. Again I persuade the manager to have me play and entertain a mob of diners mostly made up of friends. I don't know enough songs so bring in a synthesiser player and together we work up some poems set to music to flesh out the set. When I arrive I discover the waitress in the restaurant is the girl on the bus I waved at on my first day at secondary school and for years afterwards. She is a couple of years older than me and our friends have not mixed, so until this moment we have never been in the same place at the same time. I stand in the doorway, speechless at the coincidence of her presence, while she rushes about setting the tables. We acknowledge each other with a smile and I attempt to start a conversation by repeating my little boy wave, which she ignores. I begin with the Neil Young song 'Helpless', repeating the opening chords until I am sure I have the attention of everyone in the restaurant. The waitress is standing behind the counter watching me. I do not have a girlfriend and since I arrived tonight have been thinking what an amazing story it would be if we got together after all these years, her wooed by my music. I sing the opening line to the audience while watching, out of the corner of my eye, the waitress with her big eyes and long dark hair. I am only a few words into the song when I see her raise a hand to her mouth to stifle a laugh and run away to the kitchen.

It will be thirty-four years before I sing another song on stage.

Should I Stay or Should I Go, 2017

After the gig at Port Eliot normal life takes over. There are courses to teach and a job writing music for another theatre show. In October, when I run a residential writing workshop near Dumfries, my guitar comes with me and on the last night I sing a few songs as if it's the most natural thing to do. For a while I think I have done it, done what I needed to do and can put the dream to rest. Then it is 2017, and on a cold, wet Friday night I return to the Thunderbolt. I am a little way from the entrance when I hear it first, the guitar riff that opens 'Should I Stay or Should I Go' by the Clash. The sound hits me like a drug that goes straight to my head, just like it did when I first heard the song in 1982. I push into the bar, packed with teenagers jumping and leaping in front of the stage, and edge my way into the crowd. Tonight is very special, because the musician playing the riff is my son, Fred. He has just turned seventeen and his guitar – my old electric guitar I bought in Bond Street with Dad – is slung low around his neck. I watch him with a sense of awe and wonder how this is even possible. Fred is quietly charismatic without recourse to the theatrical displays and facial grimacing that I was prone to at his age. The band are finding their way, discovering what they are capable of and their young audience are on the journey with them.

Then, a few weeks later I arrive at a recording studio in the railway arches beneath Waterloo station in London with Poppy. After she went to university, Poppy learned to play the drums, and with her friend Yasmin's electric guitar and punky vocals they have formed a duo and are going to make a demo. They are both nervous and feel suddenly exposed playing the song in front of a sound engineer, the first time they have performed outside the comfort of a rehearsal room. I watch from behind the glass as they ease into the session, finding their way into the song until they deliver a performance that fizzes with energy. I sit with them as the song is mixed, enjoying their exhilaration as they hear themselves, for the first time, back through studio speakers. I feel their excitement too, and it makes me realise my own journey isn't over yet.

Time After Time, 1986

It's strange how time can pass. Months turn into years and years into decades. I no longer know any songs all the way through. I carry around fragments half learned, fragments half written. Even when I get a job at the BBC and sit in studios, a few feet from my heroes singing their songs, the effect is always to silence the song in me.

Like when I go to a rehearsal studio in West London to interview Roger Waters, because he is about to take *The Wall* on tour. He comes to meet me in reception and asks if I am in a hurry. When I say I am not, he leads me into the studio, pulls out a chair, and sits me in front of an all-star band who perform the whole show, just for me.

Like when I invite Richard Thompson to record the music for a play I am directing. For years I have been going to see him in concert halls and now here he is right in front of me, in a little studio in Broadcasting House, playing what I ask him to.

Like when I make a programme with Neil Tennant of the Pet Shop Boys and he suggests we meet at the *Top of the Pops* studio, so I go there at last and watch a rehearsal where the bands pretend to perform and the applause is piped through speakers. Everything seems much, much smaller than I imagined it would be.

Like when Ian Dury sits me down in his flat in Hampstead, rolls me a big joint, then plays a rough mix of what will be his final album.

Then when I leave the BBC and start writing plays for a living and have a parallel life writing music and songs for theatre shows, they are always songs for other people to sing and I forget them as soon as the show is over.

As I get older it gets harder to be a beginner again, especially beginning something as revealing as singing. Occasionally, over the years, when I am alone, I will write and record a song on my old four-track Portastudio, but will play it to almost no one, because when I sing, I expose parts of my self that are kept hidden. There is such a fear of looking stupid, of public ridicule, of the facade crumbling and what is within found wanting. It is the fear of failure that stops me from trying.

And time passes. And in 2000 Dad contracts lung cancer and dies the next year. But when I reach for the guitar to sing how it feels, it is only fragments I find.

And time passes.

Weeks. Months. Years. Decades.

Until that moment on the Isles of Scilly where my story begins again.

Walk With You Again, 2017

A couple of days after the studio session under Waterloo station, I am messing around on the internet when I come across a recording of an old concert by Everything But The Girl, the duo of Tracey Thorn and Ben Watt. They provided a soundtrack to my twenties and thirties, developing from jazzy, acoustic songs and cult status to electronica and worldwide hits. Now on my computer screen I am watching a close-up of Ben Watt's left hand and see a couple of chords I don't recognise. I go out to the kitchen and try them. Suddenly, it is as if a gateway opens beyond which is a song demanding to be heard. It starts with a memory: I am standing by my dad's grave with my son Fred, who asks what I would do if I could spend another day with my father. We would go to Golden Cap in Dorset, the highest hill on the South Coast. The song becomes the story of the day I imagine us having together. I play it to Sarah, without any preamble, and see tears in her eyes when I finish.

This, this is what a song can do.

*

'Walk With You Again'

As we walk away
From the B&B
Out towards the sea
Up on Golden Cap
Following the map
That's written in your head

You close your eyes and face the sea
Breathing deeply saying here I feel free
It's days like this that make life worth living

High up on the hill
We look out to Portland Bill
While I talk about the past
How I made nothing last
You say there's nothing wrong
The past it has all gone
Let's just enjoy the view

There's so much that I want to say
So little time before you go away
So many questions needing answers
(Chorus)
On this precious day
I will chase all the shadows in my tiny world away
So I can listen to every single word that you say
As I walk with you again
As I walk with you again

Now we're sitting down
Close together on the ground
I feel the warmth of your skin
See the stubble on your chin
With the wind upon my face
I feel your hesitant embrace
When I put my arms around you

Remember how I used to shake your hand
That's what I thought you did when you were a man
Come on close now I'm all for hugging

Then we're spinning round
As we're running down
Stopping by the windblown tree
It's when you look at me
I say what do you see

269

You say we can agree
We're a lot like each other

I like to feel the wood grain beneath my hand
That is what I understand
You're using words but you're still building castles
(Chorus)
It's when we get down to the beach that you start slipping out
        of reach
It's like you're drifting out to sea, scattered far away from me
But before you leave this day I want you to hear me say
You might be gone but you're not forgotten
(Chorus)

On the Road Again, 2017

It is not over. I know that after I write 'Walk With You Again', because other songs start to come too. I never sit down to write; there is always the same sense of a gateway opening and a song demanding to be heard. I write about an abortive trip my grandfather made to Australia to become a sheep farmer; I write about the sensation of moving home as my house is soon to be sold and I will move away from Bristol; I write about the beach in Hythe and going there to shout into the wind; I write about insomnia. The more songs I write, the more I know I will have to carry on playing them.

It's Only Just Begun, 1972

In my last year at primary school, Mum, Dad and I go on holiday for two weeks to a Cornish cottage in a seaside village called Trevone. I remember this holiday vividly, because it is the first time we have been away for so long and two weeks feels like for ever. This is the age before motorways, so it takes us all night to get there, driving across the full width of England in our little Morris Traveller, me sleeping stretched out on the back seat, waking with the dawn. Then, the landscape is strange: wide, sweeping valleys in Devon and the rocky outcrops of Cornwall. After we arrive the sun shines every single day as we walk on the clifftops and swim in sparkling, cold sea. It is this holiday feeling I imagined it would be like on the road, going from town to town, cut loose from the tedium of everyday life. In the cottage, my bed is a bunk on the landing and Dad comes to find me each morning on his way to make early morning tea.

Nearing the end of the holiday, I ask him, 'Is it over yet?'

Dad always replies by saying exactly the same thing, even on the last day, as we are about to pack our suitcases for the long drive back to Kent. 'No,' he says. 'It's only just begun.'

And that is exactly how I feel today, out on the road not taken.

'On the Road Not Taken'

It was on a golden morning
I headed for the door
Took my leave of everything
I'd ever known before
The world was like a flower
Opening in spring
As I walked away from home that day
I began to sing

I sang about the road I took
And the people that I met
I sang about the good times
I sang about regret
But the song was in my head
I couldn't sing out loud
So the music faded
As I melted in the crowd

(Chorus)
I'm on the road not taken
I'm staking out my claim
I won't wait for the storm to pass
I'm going to dance in the rain
Dance in the rain

Once it started raining
I'd hide myself away
I thought there'd be tomorrow
There'd be another day
The glitter and the glory
Seemed like prizes to be won
I thought if I kept my head down
I could please everyone

It was never easy
Telling right from wrong
But the road was the clearest
Didn't stop the song
For so long it felt as though
There was no right to choose
Until the parting of the ways
There was nothing left to lose
(Chorus)

A Tour Diary, 2017

In his gig diary, *The Road Beneath My Feet*, Frank Turner gets right to the heart of the troubadour dream when he says, 'To be on the move in distant places, seeing new, strange, wonderful things, experiencing new things and encountering new people – that's the stuff of life to me.' I would add to this that normally, when I am going somewhere I am usually so absorbed by what I am about to do that I hardly look out of the window of the train that is taking me there. When I am going to sing, I cannot do anything else, so stare through the windows of trains, buses and cars and talk to the people around me. I actually experience the world differently.

The book you are now reading is funded by subscription and in 2017 it becomes clear I need to find more subscribers. The way to do this? Go back out on the road and perform in the living rooms of anyone who will have me and can pull together a small audience of like-minded people.

Long ago, in my first year at Brockhill, I had an art teacher called Mr Hyde. I remember he wore a grey jacket and had a long, pointy beard. There was a big metal sculpture outside the main hall that was said to be a piece of modern art, with angular shapes pointing skyward. None of us could understand what it was supposed to be. One day, Mr Hyde led us out of the classroom and sat us around the sculpture.

'Don't draw it,' he said. 'Draw what is around and in between. That way you'll learn more about the thing itself.' At the time I didn't know what he was talking about. But now I do. So in the account of the tour that follows, I have drawn a bit of the sculpture, but a lot of what is around it too.

13 July 2017, Bristol

I have this idea for small-scale gigs in people's houses. No amplification: just my guitar, some stories and me. A friend suggests I try out the idea with her book club and fixes up a date in July. I sold my house and moved to Cardiff two weeks ago and this is my first time back in Bristol. Tonight I will play in a large Victorian house, in a big kitchen with bifolding doors that open onto a long garden; a secret world in the heart of the city. It is a warm evening and everyone is outside, the garden full of smart-looking people drinking prosecco and eating canapés. The performance anxiety is present, but very much in the background, so before I play, I take a guided tour of the garden and take in most of what I am told, which would have been impossible last year. Most of the audience have a few drinks and are in a good mood when I start. They are scattered on seats and sofas that face me, with the garden behind, so there is something else to look at if they get bored. I start well, with an instrumental, then introduce the first song. I say that since beginning this quest, I have been trying to work out what sort of vocalist I am and have decided I am a punk-folk singer. Halfway through 'Brislington Diamonds', I forget the words and grind to a halt. It is the perfect opportunity to try out the new strategy for when things go wrong. I talk about all the mistakes I have seen other people make in the last couple of years and how they have improved the shows, which gets a laugh. I do not forget any other lyrics but am aware it has been a long time since I last played live. When I sing 'Walk With You Again', a man in the room starts to cry. I decide to set up a whole tour in the autumn. Once again I ask for help via social media and people respond with offers of living rooms and beds for the night.

25 September 2017, Axminster

I leave home with my small guitar and a backpack. I am nervous again and sleeping badly. Stepping into the taxi under a brooding sky, I am overwhelmed by a wave of tiredness that lasts from Cardiff to somewhere in the middle of Somerset, where the train crashes into a shopping trolley. The driver gets out to have a look. Despite a terrifying metallic screech, there is no damage and we carry on. Now I am fully awake. From Exeter to Axminster I stare out of the window, watching Devon fields stepping way northwards under gigantic clouds and trees casting long shadows in late afternoon sunshine.

Pete picks me up at Axminster station and drives me to the cottage where he lives with his wife, Wendy. They are the hosts of tonight's gig and where I will stay the night, in a house cocooned in a tree-lined valley. There is a log fire burning in the living room, already set with chairs for tonight. After dinner, I go to my room to tune the guitar and warm up my voice. When I come down again, the audience have arrived. It is lovely to travel light and play without amplification, but a living room full of people deadens the sound and maybe it is this, or maybe it is the tiredness, but halfway through 'Poppysong' I forget the words. I make my speech about mistakes and someone suggests I sing 'la la la' until I get to a bit I do remember. I follow this advice and it works. People join in and sing when asked and by the end it feels special, sitting around the fire in this cottage, deep in the woods. Before going to bed I stand on the balcony outside my bedroom and look up to see bats and the winking lights of aircraft. Then as my eyes adjust to the night the Milky Way appears, stretching across the sky to where it vanishes in the dark silhouettes of trees.

26 September 2017, *Portland*

I wake early and lie still, enjoying the deep silence of the woods outside my bedroom. When it is light I lift the blind to see the hills shrouded in a fine mist. There is such a sense of peace in this place and the welcome so warm, it is hard to say goodbye. Pete drives me through the Dorset countryside to Bridport where I will catch a bus to the next gig. We drive past Golden Cap, the hill that features in 'Walk With You Again', my song about spending one more day with my late father. I remember how Dad would stand tall and breathe deeply, smiling at a view that takes in Portland Bill to the east and the cliffs of the Devon coast tapering westward. As we drive along the A35, I show Pete the B&B where we used to stay in the village of Morcombelake. It is not a B&B any more, but as we flash past, I see in the window Rose, the landlady, looking out at the view. She still lives there and even after all these years I recognise her at once.

I have forty minutes before my bus, so walk up the High Street, bustling and warm in the late September sun, enjoying the liminal space between arrival and departure, having nothing to do but wait and savour the absence of anxiety.

The sun is hot now and it feels like the holidays on Weymouth seafront. Then Emma collects me, her eighteen-month-old son Patrick fast asleep in a car seat. This afternoon I am playing at the Brackenbury Centre, a community hall on the Isle of Portland. There is a delicious sea smell in the air and a rich, lively acoustic in this big room. I run through songs then arrange the chairs in a semicircle in the middle of the hall as Emma lays out quiches and cakes. The audience arrive and are handed mugs of hot tea. Among the audience are several small children who sit with plates of food, listening attentively to my stories of small-town life in the 1970s. Near the end, Patrick, overcome with curiosity, toddles up close to investigate the guitar.

Then it is over and I am at Weymouth station. I step on to an almost empty train with a bag full of quiche, crisps and cake. I watch the South Coast disappear into shadows and darkness as we rumble along the line towards Southampton. When I was eighteen and imagining life on the road I never thought it would be like this. But I like it. I like the quiche and cake and the audiences who listen carefully. And I like the moments in between, moments like this, when I have nothing to do but sit and look and think.

11 October 2017, The Thunderbolt, Bristol

Newport station looks bleak this rain-soaked afternoon as I step off the delayed Cardiff train and discover I have missed my connection. The anxiety has returned with a vengeance. Avoiding water cascading through holes in the roof, I make my way to a bench next to the closed-down WHSmith kiosk. Next to me is an old man I have never met before wearing washed-out fleecy trousers. He looks at me for a moment then raises his hand, inviting a high five. When I return the gesture he snatches his hand away and puts it up against his eye like a pretend telescope. Then he spots my guitar and asks if I know someone he knows who lives in Chepstow who also plays the guitar.

In Bristol I mount the guitar on my back and wheel my bag through sheeting rain to an Airbnb near the Thunderbolt in Totterdown. The last few hundred yards involve climbing the steepest residential street in Britain. My bedroom is a cubbyhole at the top of stairs leading onto a roof terrace. The rain has stopped and the sun is setting. I stand, mesmerised by the view. I can see Clifton, Brandon Hill, the Suspension Bridge; navigation marks of my former home.

When I last came to the Thunderbolt, it was to see my son Fred play to a mosh pit full of leaping teenagers. Tonight as I soundcheck, Dave the landlord sets out rows of chairs on the dance floor. There will be no leaping tonight. I go out into the garden and force myself to eat two readymade salads.

Dave gives me the signal. It is time. I crunch over broken glass on the floor of the dressing room and out onto the stage. In the audience is Sarah, my children, my children's mum and friends from all corners of life. Somehow, the stakes seem higher when the audience is known and maybe that is why I am so anxious again. They are all out there now, just visible in the gloom beyond the stage lights. I play the first notes, right on the edge of forgetting everything, but I make it through the first couple of numbers and gradually the anxiety eases. As I relax, I realise it is a lovely thing to be playing to a room radiating so much goodwill. Afterwards both Fred and Poppy, who seem genuinely moved by what they heard tonight, hug me. Such moments are rare and precious.

Sarah and I are last out of the Thunderbolt. Dave locks

the door behind us and we walk along wet pavements, up the steep hill, then climb the stairs to our cubbyhole. It is so small we take turns to undress. With the light off it feels as though we are almost in the clouds.

12 October 2017, Winchester

Late afternoon sun on the meadows of the Itchen Valley highlights a blaze of autumn colour. The train approaches Winchester. It was on an autumn day thirty-five years ago I came here to begin a degree in Drama, Theatre and Television Studies. By then I had stopped singing in front of people. Although I became immersed in recording and played the guitar whenever I could, I never actually sang a song in public. Now I am back and playing at Winchester University and that feels important.

We are a small group who gather in the Terrace Bar of the Student Union. This is a new building on the site of the old refectory. As I look out of the window behind me I remember the view from three decades ago, when we poured tea from giant urns, served with bread and butter and trays of homemade cakes. David, who was in the year above me and now runs the university bookshop, has organised this evening. We met again a few years ago when I came to speak at the Winchester Writers' Festival and he has supported this project right from the start. Also in the audience are Deb and Paddy, old friends from university days. They order a bottle of wine and settle in the front row. We ease into banter that feels like a conversation interrupted in the 1980s.

I am perched on a little stage and even though there are not many of us, everyone sings along when asked and it feels like a proper gig, until it ends and we all leave together.

The next morning I walk through the water meadows and up St Catherine's Hill, the Iron Age hill fort that overlooks the city. I came here on my first week in 1982, intoxicated by new friends and independence. It felt as though the world was opening up before me. And that's what it is like today as I head to another gig, with a guitar on my back and a head full of all the songs I didn't sing.

13 October 2017, Bishopstoke, Hampshire

I lift my bag down the footbridge stairs at Eastleigh station and see Glen on the other side of the ticket barriers. He is wearing an exotic hat, sporting a white beard and holding a walking stick. It is more than thirty years since we last met and we have both changed, but I recognise him right away. We head to town in search of a taxi. As we travel back home Glen tells me about the years in between and his diagnosis of the neurological movement disorder, dystonia. The symptoms can resemble those of Parkinson's disease and that is what Glen thought he had, until a privately arranged brain scan revealed something different.

Glen's wife Sian opens the front door. Sian is another friend from university days and in a convoluted way, I was responsible for the circumstances of their meeting in the late eighties. And here they are three decades later, still together with two grown-up children.

The furniture has been rearranged so the living room resembles a bohemian arts club. I will be under a light at one end, looking down the room that has been set theatre style with sofas and chairs. In my upstairs bedroom, I warm up with the guitar as the first guests arrive. I hear the clink of glasses and the sound of laughter and just know it is going to be a good evening; I can tell from a distance when people are up for it.

It is still hard to know what to do with the last minutes before performing. Although anxiety is much reduced and is only a background murmur tonight, I still don't feel like chatting, so wander in and out, breathing deeply and keeping on the move.

It is a lovely night, exactly the sort of thing I hoped would happen when I decided to do this. Everybody gets it and it all makes sense. There is laughter, applause and plenty of joining in. We are all in it together, so there is no division between performer and audience and because I am not amplified, when I ask people to sing, they are as loud as me.

14 October 2017, Salcombe
At Eastleigh I put on headphones and disappear into my own world, missing an announcement that says my train has changed destination. That is why, after a diversionary

ride through Hampshire, I end up in the Upper Crust on Southampton Central with an hour to spare, sitting by the window eating a mozzarella and tomato baguette. The first time I came here was in 1983 on my way to Radio Solent where I was about to be interviewed about my – recorded on cassette tape – music. I was young and nervous as this was the first time I had spoken live on air. A friend happened to have his car radio on and was so startled to hear my voice, he circled a roundabout four times.

I wait until the train has left Southampton before I put on my headphones again, then look out of the window as we pass from the fields of Hampshire to the wide open spaces of Wiltshire, the flatlands of Somerset and down to where the line follows the Devon coast at Dawlish, where the tide is in and the sea calm under drab grey Saturday skies.

Anne picks me up at Totnes and drives me to her home in Salcombe. Somewhere in between the sun comes out but I don't notice as I am so busy talking, then being introduced to Anne's artist husband Stephen, then discovering his paintings lining the walls, so I am not prepared for what I see when I am taken onto the balcony. We are high up on a hillside overlooking the town and the view is incredible. Patchwork fields taper to the distance; wooded slopes drop to the estuary; yachts are tethered to moorings in still water; all of this under piercing blue sky that seems to have come from nowhere. The whole house is full of light with stunning vistas from every window. I take advantage of the late-afternoon lull to walk down the steep hill to the waterside and linger in the holiday atmosphere of the town. Back at the house, Sarah arrives from Cardiff and I lead her onto the balcony to show her the view.

Anne and Stephen are having a party tonight. Guests arrive and cluster in the kitchen, eating and drinking. I can't engage in conversation, so disappear into my room to tinker with the guitar, then lie still, listening to distant chatter. It is a wonderful thing to be, at last, without anxiety and I wonder if repetition is the key. The party splits in two with those who want to carry on drinking – and who can blame them – staying in the kitchen. The rest of us assemble in the living room and I begin.

Afterwards, Sarah and I walk to the town and sit outside a pub, enjoying the sensation that the work of the day is done. Back at the house most people have gone, but someone asks if I will play some more. The evening ends with Sarah and a party guest dancing to the song about my grandfather who went to Australia to be a sheep farmer after the First World War, but came back again when my grandmother refused to join him. It is good to think his adventures are fuelling mine, here in Devon, a hundred years down the line.

20 October 2017, Canterbury

It is four in the afternoon and the low sun casts long shadows on the platform of Sandling station in Kent. I came down yesterday to see Mum and am now en route to Canterbury to play in another living room. Last night, at home, I sang to Mum, which I have never done before. It was so odd to sing a song about my late father directly to my mother. She cannot hear well and because the song is loud and quick, a lot of it passed her by, but afterwards she told me she enjoyed listening and gave me a hug.

At Ashford I change trains and jump into the next carriage with great confidence, swinging my guitar like a seasoned troubadour. I look out at the dusk and think how the fields of Kent all look the same, until the conductor checks my ticket and tells me they are actually the same fields I saw moments ago. The train split at Ashford and I got onto the wrong half. I go back to Sandling and wait in the cold for forty-five minutes.

Vicky collects me from Canterbury West. Beyond her front door I peer into a room off the corridor and see saxophones, belonging to Vicky's partner, Eduard. I spot an opportunity.

Since the experience on the Isles of Scilly last year when I missed a meal, I have been making sure I eat before each show and when I do, any residual anxiety decreases. We share a mushroom risotto and my warmth and certainty returns. Then, after testing the acoustics in the living room I disappear until it is time to begin.

One of the songs I am playing every night is 'Thunder Road' by Bruce Springsteen; a story with a dark heart that can be quietly told. The protagonist in the song is getting older in the same old town and believes he can escape himself on the open road. There is a woman called Mary who has been left behind as well, and he watches her dancing on a porch, before trying to persuade her to come away too. At the end of the song is a sax riff, played on the record by the late Clarence Clemons. With a saxophonist in the house it seems too good an opportunity to miss, so at the end of the song Eduard appears at the other end of the room, surprising the audience with the sax line and improvising around it. The music soars and lifts, and there is a wonderful moment of connection, one instrument responding to another in the warp and weft of collaboration.

The sound plays on in my head as I get back on the train with the drunks and partygoers to travel back through the dark fields of Kent, to Mum's house and the welcome of the room from which once I was so desperate to escape.

21 October 2017, Bridport

On the train to London I put my hand in my backpack and find a layer of crushed cake. On this tour I am forever being given little parcels of food that find their way to the bottom of my bag and disintegrate. I recognise the icing from a gig over two weeks ago. On the train to Taunton I am staring at the landscape, thinking I have never seen the progress of autumn so clearly before, when it strikes me how lucky I am to be making this journey. There was never any possibility my grandad could do this and today I learned my mother was never allowed to begin. I took her out for coffee before catching the train and she told me she played the recorder so well, a teacher wanted her to apply for a scholarship at music school. My grandfather wouldn't hear of it, so she left at fifteen and went to work in a solicitor's office.

At Taunton station I rendezvous with Sarah who drives me to a village outside Bridport in Dorset. Maya welcomes me into her country home and feeds me scrambled eggs on toast. At the end of 'Boulder to Birmingham', in the moment before the applause begins, I hear a tiny appreciative sigh. It is a sound I have heard at poetry readings and classical concerts and am hearing more and more on this tour. It is so subtle that when I am amplified it doesn't register, but in a living room it is audible. There is usually only one person making the noise, it is often a woman and I cannot always tell who made it, but it is such a satisfying thing to hear, because it is the sound of someone being moved by what they have heard. And when you have one person with you early on then it is likely that the feeling will spread through the crowd.

24 October 2017, Cheltenham

I am collected from home by an Uber driver who wants to know if there is a musical instrument in my guitar-shaped case. When I say it is an acoustic guitar he asks if playing it is making me good money. I can't face telling the whole story so say no, not really. He tells me about musicians in Nigeria, his home country, going from wedding to wedding and coming home with wheelbarrows full of cash. He thinks I should do the same in the UK. 'You got to make dollar, bruv,' he says.

Then I am standing next to my guitar on Cardiff Central station waiting for the 16:45 to Cheltenham Spa. The platform is lined with homeward-bound commuters as I go out to work. Any musician will know this comes with the territory, but after decades of daytime working it is still strange to have to be at my best at night.

31 October 2017, Snowdonia

I pack for five days and end up with a bag almost too heavy to lift. Outside it is unseasonably warm, but from the train everything looks as it should: brown ploughed fields, stubble, high clouds and banks of trees, golden and green. We travel along the coast of North Wales. To my left are glimpses of mountains and to my right the Irish Sea.

Lun is waiting on the platform at Bangor. We drive into the countryside and twenty minutes later turn off the main road into the mountains, then along a lane in a valley, once the route of a mine railway. The cottage, where Lun lives with her husband Pete, used to be home to the engine driver. Tonight is Halloween and there will be a party at which I will play. The kitchen is a hive of activity as Halloween-themed food – eyeballs made from quail eggs and half a small tomato – is created and laid on plates. I crave mountain air, so walk back along the road, stopping to explore a disused engine shed, singing 'Coal Not Dole' in the roofless chamber.

Broken slates lie on the grassy floor, and ivy grows around cavities where the doors used to be.

It is dark when I return and the cottage lights are on so everything seems warm and welcoming. I practise in the living room and the wooden floor and thick cottage walls make for a supportive acoustic. A table light beside me casts giant shadows on the wall. It seems just right for Halloween.

The first people arrive when I am upstairs in my room. Everyone is in costume, and waves of laughter build with each new guest, as someone with fangs for teeth, or an axe through the head, steps into the kitchen. Menna, who came to see me in Berlin, is the last to arrive and is without fancy dress.

I walk into the kitchen, but sensing the performance ahead, can't join in with the fun. I take a plate of macaroni cheese and a glass of water up to my room and eat without tasting, then lie on the bed, fiddle with the guitar and wait. The partygoers are having so much fun with the costumes and the food that my start is delayed. Then there is a knock on the door and I pick up my guitar, strap a miniature witch's hat on my head and walk into a living room full of ghouls and ghosts, sitting in semi-darkness.

When I reach to the encore and sing 'Puff, the Magic Dragon', I see a man wiping tears from his face. He tells me afterwards the song unlocked long-buried memories and feelings, taking him back to forgotten childhood landscapes, just like it does with me. Once again, we become a little community and people tell me their own stories late into the night. Menna is staying here too and we chat for a while. She has enjoyed this evening, the people coming together and listening to songs and stories in the dark. 'It's unusual,' she says, 'like you're doing something very new, when actually you're doing something very old.' It makes me think of my grandad and his band in their back parlour on a Friday night. Maybe I am rediscovering a tradition that skipped a generation.

1 November 2017, Southport

Next day I travel back along the coast to Chester, where I change trains for Liverpool. As I am waiting for the Liverpool connection I realise there is no toilet on my platform. This is significant, as carefully planned loo stops have become an important part of the smooth running of this tour. I trace the route to the loo with my eyes and see two staircases and a footbridge. Because of the big bag and guitar, I gamble there will be a toilet on board. We travel north through unfamiliar country lit up by bright winter sunshine. Hooton, Spital, Port Sunlight; I enjoy the names and try not to think about my growing discomfort. When this is impossible I ask a passing guard for the location of the loo. There isn't one. As we approach Liverpool, I look out across the Mersey to the Liver Building and the cathedral. I change at Moorfields, but there is no time to navigate my way out of the maze of underground tunnels before the Southport train arrives. Now I cannot think of anything else but the need to wee.

There is Wi-Fi available on the platform so I use this great technological innovation to search for 'toilets + Merseyrail trains'. I learn that no Merseyrail trains have toilets. There are forty-five minutes to go. When we emerge from the tunnel I look out at docks and industrial buildings and stand up, sit down, cross my legs, uncross them and stand up again. Bank Hall, Bootle Oriel Road, Bootle New Strand. There are fourteen stops between Moorfields and Southport and I feel every one, hearing the platform sounds of each station after we stop, urging the doors to close and the train to move again. Hall Road, Hightown, Formby, it seems to take for ever. Linda and her friend Sally are waiting beyond the barrier at Southport. I met them both when I was teaching at a writer's conference earlier in the year, but now is not the time for a big reunion. I drop my luggage at their feet and run for the loo, which is actually behind the ticket barriers and requires further, painful negotiation.

Because Sally is in the spare room, Linda has put me up in a nearby B&B. I am shown to my room by the owner, Max, a man who speaks with proprietorial confidence and, I get the impression, doesn't suffer fools gladly. Max looks as if he might have been a boxer in a former life and I wouldn't fancy my chances if, say, I got pissed, lost my keys and turned up banging on the front door in the middle of the night. He explains in great detail how everything works. I realise, halfway through the section concerned with the idiosyncrasies of the plumbing, I have been so focused on appearing not to be a fool, I have not listened to a single word he has said. Subsequently, I never manage to switch the television on and will spend ten minutes tomorrow trying to make hot water come out of the shower. Eventually, the talk turns to what I am doing. I say I am in the middle of a living-room tour and am singing tonight. Max tells me about a Gary Barlow tribute act who stays at the B&B. Apparently the tribute looks so like the real Gary Barlow that a wave of starstruck excitement passes through the breakfast room when he comes in for his Full English. Max wonders if I am doing something similar? I say no, I am a punk-folk singer. This acts as a full stop to our conversation and Max heads from the room telling me not to be shy in asking for more teabags and milk capsules, should I require them.

There is time for a walk before the show tonight so I head out into the early evening. It is satisfyingly cold and my coat is buttoned up against the wind. There is a moment of sunset through distant clouds when I experience the slightly discombobulated sense of being in an American city, here on these straight, wide boulevards. The pier is closed but I stand on the sea wall and look across the bay to Blackpool Tower, lit up on the horizon.

On the way back I pass Southport Theatre and Convention Centre where the blues guitarist John Mayall is playing tonight. From outside I hear the band soundcheck and feel a sense of brotherhood for all of us out on the road, even though they are playing to a packed convention centre and I am singing for my supper in a living room.

2 November 2017, *Ripon*

From the TransPennine Express, I watch Yorkshire valleys and towns built on steep-sided hills. There are high clouds and no sun. At Leeds a Chinese man who speaks no English and wants to go to Wakefield approaches me. There are, I discover, two stations in Wakefield and I am trying to establish which one he wants when he spots someone more promising and runs away. I sit with my guitar in the cycle space on the way to Harrogate and observe the country become rolling hills, fields and woods. At Harrogate I transfer to a bus, where a delicate balancing act is required, the bag going into a luggage space and the guitar wedged between me and the seat in front. I have arranged to meet Maggie, tonight's host, at a McDonald's on a roundabout on the outskirts of Ripon. She takes me to her house that looks out over open fields. The living room is set up like a miniature theatre and looks lovely. Last night I called Mum, and when I told her I was heading for Ripon, she said she'd just received a phone call from some old friends who also lived there and wondered if the two were connected. Jean and Don had been regular visitors to our house when I was a teenager, Don being a colleague of Dad's at work, but I have not seen them since Dad's funeral in 2001. Over tea and cake

I mention their names to Maggie, who can't believe it, as they live right around the corner. So Maggie calls and asks if they would like to come along. It was just a coincidence; they had no idea I was going to be in town. When I start, there they are, sitting in the front row, a living link between the past and the present.

3 November 2017, Henfield

Tonight's gig is in Sussex, so at Leeds station I settle into my seat to look out of the window all the way to London. It gives me time to think. There are two dates left and the tour is going really well. There is something magical about playing to a room of strangers, the evening beginning with people wondering what they have let themselves in for, me gradually winning them over with songs and stories. Most people seem to enjoy it. Most people, but not everyone.

There was the strange case of the man in the blue patterned shirt. Gigs in small rooms are so intimate that I see everybody in the audience. There are usually some people who really love it, some who think it's OK and a couple who don't mind either way. Afterwards, most of the audience will say something positive, or at least say goodbye and good luck. The man in the blue patterned shirt disappears as soon as the gig is over, only to reappear in the car of the person giving me a lift to the station. We have a stilted conversation in which the show is never mentioned and in the long gaps in between, he sings under his breath. When I clamber out of the car, he doesn't wish me luck.

Then there was the clapping incident. At one gig in a crowded room, a couple take a nearby armchair; her sitting down, him squatting on the arm of the same chair. I notice early on that when others laugh, she does not. To begin with, she claps at the end of songs, though it is the minimum needed to remain within the realm of politeness. Eventually, she stops clapping altogether and, at the end of a song, raises her arm, so her hand is placed between her partner's hands as they clap.

And then there was the groaning woman. It is the start of a gig, the hardest part of the show. Nobody knows who I am or what to expect, so I have a few minutes to establish the evening will consist of music and talking, some of it will be funny and it is OK to heckle me. I have played my instrumental and am a few sentences in to the opener when the woman groans. It isn't a sigh or an accidental noise, but a proper, full-throated groan, the sort of sound you might make to someone you know very well, who is telling a story you have heard a hundred times before. The groan doesn't show on her face and she never makes the noise again, but for the rest of the night I am waiting for it to happen.

In my fantasy life as a troubadour, everybody loves me. The reality is most people like it but some do not. The more of this I do, the less that seems to matter. And then there is stage fright. That has melted away over the last days, but who is to say if that is a permanent state of being? I suspect performance anxiety is something I will always live with and the secret will be to channel it into the show.

My old friend Charlie meets me at Haywards Heath station. I am a little apprehensive when she tells me that most of the audience for tonight's show are musicians. I play in her kitchen, sitting on the table with my feet on a nursery chair. Right in front of me is an orchestral conductor who has performed in the Albert Hall. During the interval, he asks me about a chord he didn't recognise and is very complimentary, so I relax. When we all sing 'Puff, the Magic Dragon', there is a three-part harmony in the chorus.

4 November 2017, Hove

I save the best until last. I am in the house of my friends Sue and Edward playing in a softly lit living room lined with bookshelves. At the end of the first set, I tell the story of going to see Fred and him teaching me the guitar chords for 'Wild Thing'. I say that Fred is here tonight. There is a little gasp as he stands up and walks forward, holding his mandolin. Then we play 'Wild Thing' and everyone in the room sings along. Halfway through, I shout, 'Solo,' and Fred riffs around his instrument like it is 1975 all over again.

I do not sleep much that night. Somewhere in the small hours I reach for my computer and try to summarise what I have learned from this whole adventure. It is really quite simple.

*

- People are amazing. Ask for help and wonderful things happen.
- Singing together is brilliant.
- Performance anxiety is not an unstoppable force.
- If some people do not like what I do it does not matter.
- I can sing.

Related Reading

Greenlaw, Lavinia, *The Importance Of Music To Girls*, Faber & Faber, 2007

Solovitch, Sara, *Playing Scared: My Journey Though Stage Fright*, Bloomsbury, 2015

Sachs, Oliver, *Musicophilia: Tales of Music and the Brain*, Picador, 2008

Thorn, Tracey, *Naked at the Albert Hall*, Virago, 2015

Turner, Frank, *The Road Beneath My Feet*, Headline, 2015

Rhodes, James, *Instrumental*, Canongate, 2015

Acknowledgements

Thank you to everybody who gave me a gig, found me an audience, had me to stay and fed me. Without you this story would not have been told. Thank you to Kate McCall for producing the radio script that showed the way to write the book and Pier Productions and BBC Radio 4 who first put the story on air. Thank you to Jay Armstrong who allowed me to write an early version of this tale in *Elementum* Magazine and who took the photograph on the cover. Thank you to Tim Dee who offered the right advice at the right time. Thank you to my editor Scott Pack for believing in the book and to Ella Chappell and everyone at Unbound for keeping me at it.

Thank you to the Society of Authors whose grant bought me the time I sorely needed to write.

I would like to thank my mum, who has become a character on national radio and whose words now live in the pages of this book.

And Poppy and Fred, who for many years were my only (captive) audience.

And above all to Sarah, who listened patiently and allowed the story to unfold.

Unbound is the world's first crowdfunding publisher, established in 2011.

We believe that wonderful things can happen when you clear a path for people who share a passion. That's why we've built a platform that brings together readers and authors to crowdfund books they believe in – and give fresh ideas that don't fit the traditional mould the chance they deserve.

This book is in your hands because readers made it possible. Everyone who pledged their support is listed below. Join them by visiting unbound.com and supporting a book today.

Kathryn Aalto

Ingrid Adams

Miriam Akhtar

Matthew Allan

John Andrews

Jane Angell

Zoe Antoniades

Lou Apthorpe

Jay Armstrong

Norm Bailey

Roger Bailey

Ginny Baker

Nicola Banning

Maria Banos Smith

Deborah Barkham

Linda Barratt

Iris Bassett

Beatlebum

Paul Beatty

Louise Bellamy

Geoff and Juliet Bennett

Yasmin Berndt

John Biddle

Fran Bill

Lydia Birch

Pat Birch

Jayne & Mike Blatchford

Casey Bottono

Brigid Bowen

Linda Bradshaw

Paul Bradshaw

Geoff Braterman

Wendy Breckon

Tom Brereton-Downs

Steffie Broer

Aline Buckley

Paul Buckley

Mike Bullen

Andy Burden

Andrew Burns

Tanvir Bush

Lori Butterworth

Jenny Byers

Juliet Caird

Seamas Carey

Simon Caro

Lucy Catherine

Dawn Cawley

Angeline Chesters

Juan Christian

Stewart Clapp

Brenda and Terry Clare

Pip Claridge

Ant Clarke Cowell

Graham Clift

Maggie Cobbett

Richard Cobbett

Emma Cockburn

Christine Collister Miller

Frances Colville

Stephen Connolly

Frankie Conyers

Christine Cooke

Sophie Cottle

David Cowell

Robert Cox

Liz Crocker

Penny Dakin-Kiley

Lance Dann

Fred Gregory Davies

Sara Davies

Helen Dawson

Tim Dee

Angela and Kevin Deegan

Marilyn Denbigh

Pete Devonport

Fred Dodgson

Iris Dodgson

Poppy Dodgson

Stephen Dodgson

Sharon Dodgson-Smith

Jonathan Dransfield

Alastair Dunlop

Claire Duval Lewis

Simon Edwards

Mark Ellingham

Luke Emmett

Namdi Eneli

Katie Eungblut

Jonathan Eyres

Deb Falconer

Simon Fanshawe

Victoria Field

Kate Firth

Mike Fitzgerald

Kathryn Flegg

Sophie Flynn

Nick Forrest

Julia Forster

Liz Fossey

Elizabeth Friend

Gavin Fryer

Hayden Gabriel

Teresa Gallagher

Tom Galloway

Rocìo Garcìa Vèlez

Steve Gardiner

Gill Garratt

Jane Gately

Tim Gebbett

Jessica Gibbs

Kate Gill

Diana Gough

Louise Graham

Lavinia Greenlaw

Cathy Grimmer

Tommi Grover

Gillian Gustar

Sara Jane Hall

Janelle Hardacre

Shona Harris

Julia Hartnett

Melissa Hawker

Elise Heaven

Trevor Henegan

Judith Heneghan

Juliet Henham

Marcus Herbert

John Heywood-Waddington

Charlie Hoddell

David Holford

Kathy Holmes

Mark Holmes

Pamela HoneyHeart

Ann Horne

Chris Horseman

Kate Howells

Courtney Hulbert

Karen Hunt

Iain Hunter

Liz Hurst

Penny Ingram

Simon Jerrome

Josephine and Alan Johnson

Ben Jones

Mary Jowitt

Kate & Tracy

Ros Kennedy

Barbara Kershaw

Dan Kieran

Rosemary Kind & Chris Platt

Marietta Kirkbride

Shona Kitson

Simon Kitson

Wendy Knee

Gavin Knight

Ilse Lademann

Harriet Laurie

Tim LeRoy

Inga Lindegaard Osborne

David Lloyd

David Lowen

Nick Lowen

Teeny Lucy

Sara Lundie-Brown

Lee Lyford

Mags MacKean

Susannah Marriott

Barbara Marsh

Liz Mason

Pauline Mason

Fiona Matthews

Alan Mayes

Kate McAll

Louisa McDonnell

Rachel McNally

Simon & Ann Mills

John Mitchinson

Chris Monk

Arthuria Mullard

Clare Murphy

Fay Musselwhite

Carlo Navato

Daniel Neill

Malcolm Newton

Peter & Helen Nightingale

Hazel North

Mary Novakovich

Charles Ormrod

Scott Pack

Sarah Palmer

Andrew Parker

Mike and Julie Parker

Wynn Parks

Loraine Parnell

Julia Pattison

Clare Pawley

Richard Payne

Juliet and Nick Penfold

Hugo Perks

Bob Peterson

Maya Pieris

Lucy Pitman-Wallace

Justin Pollard

Carole Porter

Saskia Portway

Anna Poulton

Christina Poulton

Gill Powell

Menna Pragnell

Sue Pratt

Mary Price

Liz Purnell

Anne Rainbow

Jonathan Richards

John Riches

Eluned Roberts and Peter
    Johnson

Lynne Rodgers

Jan Rowlands

Bev & Julian Saunders

Sarah Saunders

Mike Scott Thomson

Elizabeth Seal

Alan Searl

Dolores Sheridan

Caroline Sherwood

Tina Shingler

Helen Shipman

David Simpkin

Hannah Smith

Helen Smith

Maggie Smith

Robert Smith

Janet Smithies

Miranda Steed

Merlin Stone

Sarah Stone

Adrienne Stratford

Sean Street

Super Mega Action Plus

Kerry Symington

Julie Taylor

Lorna Taylor

Paul Tebbutt

Sue Teddern and Edward
  Crask

Lindsay Trenholme

Christopher Trent

Sally Trueman Dicken

Lucy Tuck

Tilly Vacher

Tony Vanderheyden

Kris Ventris-Field

Andrew Wain

Karen Waldron

Ian Walker

Linda Walker

Jenny Walmsley

Bridget Whelan

Jeremy White

Miranda Whiting

Glen Wiffen

Sian Wiffen

Tony Wiffen

Jules Wilkinson

Jen Williams

Jenna and Steve Williams

Heidi Williamson

Derek Wilson

Kate Wilson

Kate Wiseman

Michael Stefan Wood BEM

J L Yates